TRUE CRIME STORIES OF FAIRFIELD, CALIFORNIA

TONY WADE

Published by The History Press
An imprint of Arcadia Publishing
Charleston, SC
www.historypress.com

First published 2025

Manufactured in the United States

ISBN 9781467170260

Library of Congress Control Number 2025937564

ALSO BY TONY WADE

Growing Up in Fairfield, California
Lost Restaurants of Fairfield, California
Armijo High School: Fairfield, California
Growing Up in Vacaville

All of the above are available at your local bookstore or may be ordered by visiting: www.arcadiapublishing.com

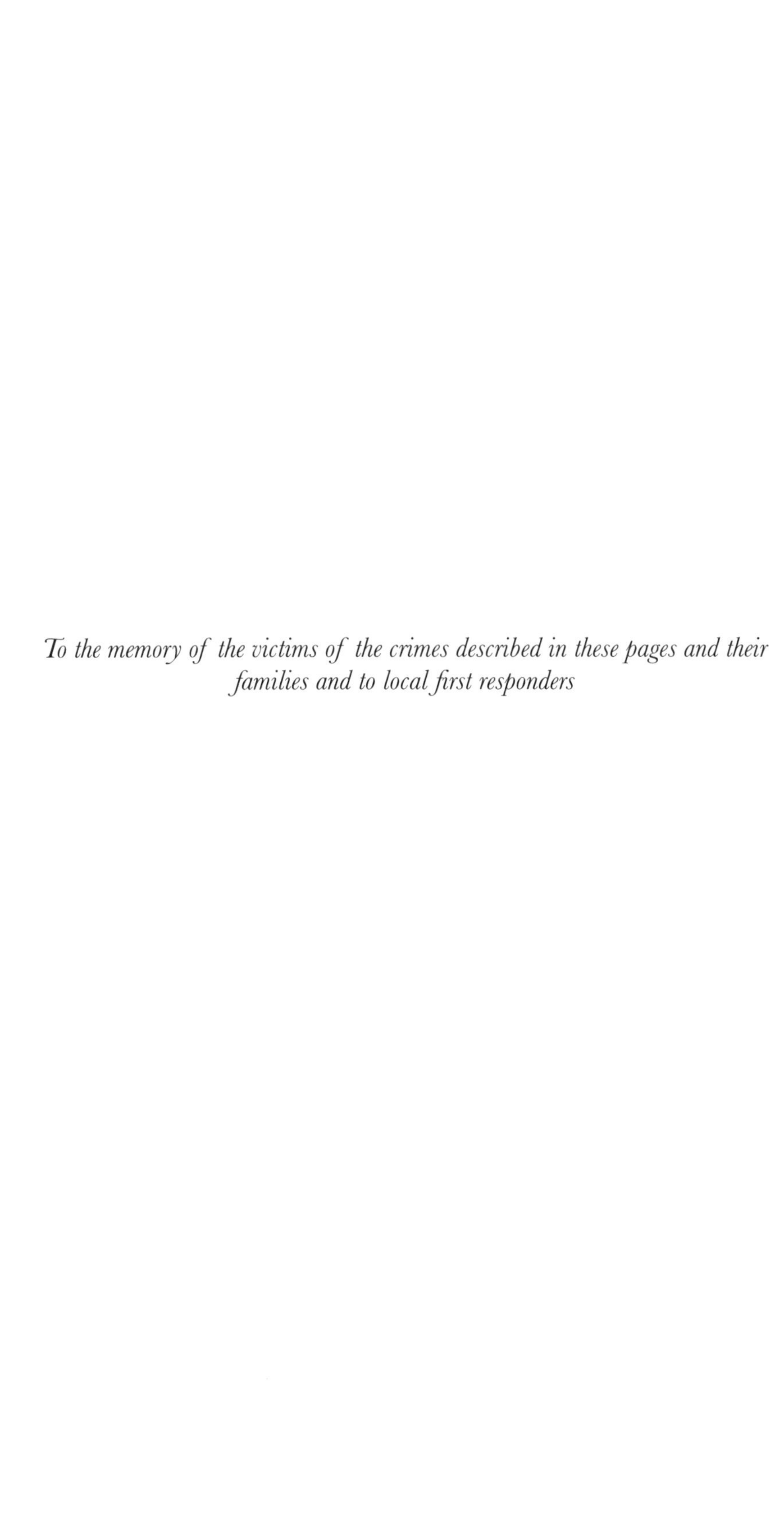

To the memory of the victims of the crimes described in these pages and their families and to local first responders

CONTENTS

PREFACE
THE IRONY OF TRUE CRIME

The infectiousness of crime is like that of the plague.
—Napoleon Bonaparte

Can I be honest? I've never really been a huge fan of the true crime genre. Only a mere handful of the seven-hundred-plus Back in the Day columns that I've written for the *Daily Republic* could be categorized as such. Still, I will say that whenever I have dipped my toes into true crime, those columns were always some of the most popular.

Which is kinda weird to me. I mean, the horror and outrage that people have about crime in their community is only equaled by their appetite for reading about it.

That local fascination is not a new thing, as reflected in a January 8, 1959 article in the *Solano Republican* newspaper, predecessor to the *Daily Republic*. It listed the most popular book genres in the Solano County library system back then. The article was titled "'Pure' Murder Rates Highest in Solano Readers' Choices."

True crime has been popular for decades, and some say it's due to a combination of factors.

One reason is that it can seem like a real-life mystery that audiences can feel invested in. The structure of a mystery, with the killer's identity revealed at the end, is also something people enjoy. It's satisfying to pretend to be a member of the Scooby-Doo Mystery Machine crew and ultimately pull the mask off the perp's face at the end of the episode. As we will see, however, in real life, crime is often much messier than fiction.

The Solano County Jail on Union Avenue in Fairfield. *Tony Wade.*

True crime can provide adrenaline rushes that are super-intense, but safe. It's a form of nonthreatening escapism and can even help some people find meaning in their lives as they seek justice for others.

I have done my best to collect a representative sampling of Fairfield true crime stories, and this is not meant to be an encyclopedic list. Many of them happened in Fairfield proper, but some have admittedly tenuous connections such as having been tried at the county courthouse downtown or somehow involving the county jail.

Just an aside: In the You Can't Make This Stuff Up Department, when I was ready to begin the research process for this book, I was stymied by—believe it or not—a true crime. On April 5, 2024, some cruel and evil tech dorks launched a ransomware attack on, of all things, the Solano County Library. The entire library computer system and internet were down for over three months! That meant that doing the tedious but often very fruitful task of sitting for hours in front of a library computer and culling crime stories from past newspapers via microfilm was out.

Fortunately, I already had extensive files, and what I didn't have was rounded out by info from that cool invention by Al Gore, the interwebs.

Of course, the most sensational stories are those that involve the ultimate crime, murder. To be sure there have been some truly horrifying examples in Fairfield's history, but I have refrained from being sensationalistic in this book. I just tell the stories.

I am also keenly aware that for family and friends of loved ones whose lives were taken, the tales presented here are not just an abstract story in a book but a traumatizing event in their lives. Be assured that I see, honor and respect them.

This book is a bit of a departure from my first four, which relied heavily on the powerful and pleasing magnetic pull of nostalgia. But history is not puppy dogs and rainbows all the time. The history of any city is going to have chapters that include darkness as well as light.

Warmly,
Tony Wade
January 31, 2025

Left: A 1945 *Crime Does Not Pay* comic book. *Public domain.*

Right: The cover of a 1961 issue of *True Detective* magazine. *Public domain.*

1
EARLY DAYS

No punishment has ever possessed enough power of deterrence to prevent the commission of crimes. On the contrary, whatever the punishment, once a specific crime has appeared for the first time, its reappearance is more likely than its initial emergence could ever have been.
—Hannah Arendt

1851: THE CAPTAIN ROBERT WATERMAN "HELL SHIP" TRIALS

What better way to kick off *True Crime Stories of Fairfield, California* than with the founder of the city, Captain Robert Waterman? In 1858, when Fairfield wrested the county seat designation away from Benicia in an election, Waterman was instrumental by pledging sixteen acres for the county buildings, plus four other blocks and $10,000.

Now there are numerous period newspaper articles about the life of Captain Waterman, and they are more accurate sources than the gushing, fanboy account that was published by *Solano Republican* newspaper editor David Weir in 1957. His book, *That Fabulous Captain Waterman*, was the result of twenty years of research, and it is quite fanciful. Parts of it read like a press release or a transcript of things a hype man would say rather than a biographer. In some sections it's like Weir tried to use every adjective from Roget's Thesaurus for *awesome* in describing Waterman.

That's not to say that the good captain hadn't racked up some pretty awesome (amazing, inspiring, extraordinary, etc.) accomplishments. He was not only a masterful skipper but also a shrewd and brilliant ship designer and rigger. Giving him his due, it is not a stretch to say he was one of the foremost geniuses in the era of sail.

As a clipper ship captain, Waterman was a speed demon. He helped design *The Sea Witch*, so named because his wife, Cordelia, purportedly once said: "To you she's a wonderful ship, but to me she's just a witch of the sea come to carry you away!"

In 1849, after heading to Hong Kong for tea, *The Sea Witch* reached New York in seventy-four days, which set a record that was not broken until 2003.

In 1851, Waterman was the skipper of *The Challenger*, a ship that was making a run from New York to San Francisco. Ads seeking crewmembers were placed in New York newspapers, and it appears that many of the men who eventually were chosen were cutthroats and well-known criminals. *That Fabulous Captain Waterman* described them as "diseased," "sub-standard" and "riffraff." By contrast, Waterman's regular crew members were described as "loyal," "capable"' and "experienced."

The hired ruffians had brought rum, whiskey, knives and guns on board. While Waterman gave the crew their instructions topside, his second mates, Jim Douglass and Hugh Patterson, tossed their goodies and weapons overboard. The living conditions on *The Challenger* were reportedly abysmal, and the crew losing their alcohol and firearms could only have exacerbated feelings of discontent.

As if that wasn't enough, dysentery ran rampant on the ship and led to the deaths of six men. Also, depending on who was telling the story, three others were lost either trying to adjust the sails in a storm or because they were not doing their jobs fast enough for Waterman and he cut a halyard (a rope that hoists the sail). Whatever the cause, they fell from the ship and drowned.

Waterman was nicknamed "Bully" and, along with his second mates, was allegedly brutal in his treatment of the crew by administering floggings (which was evidently illegal). He cut the cook's scalp with a carving knife and beat two sick sailors for working too slowly. Second mate Douglass was sadistic with his punishments of the crew, and when *The Challenger* came close to Rio de Janeiro, several crewmen mutinied. They stabbed Douglass a dozen times (which he survived), and another officer was nearly hanged.

Waterman was able to stop the mutiny. Unarmed. Evidently, he was a bit of a badass.

Waterman flogged the mutineers and had one who was discovered hiding dragged out onto the deck, broke his arm with a club and then shackled him in the sick bay by the broken arm.

When *The Challenger* arrived in San Francisco on October 29, 1851, crew members deboarded and spread the word about their side of what had transpired on their voyage. A mob of angry boatmen and sailors gathered around the vessel and were out for blood. Waterman had left the ship early in the morning, and his second mates escaped using a small boat over the side of the ship.

The mob rushed aboard the ship and were enflamed when they saw there were numerous crew members who had serious injuries. The mayor of San Francisco, with the help of several citizens, was able to get the near riot under control.

From the *New Orleans Weekly Delta*:

> *The scene at this time onboard the ship beggars all description. Five of* [the crew members] *are mangled and bruised in the most shocking manner. One poor fellow died today and five others it is expected will soon be in the embrace of death. One of the men now lying on his deathbed has been severely injured in his genitals by a kick from this brute in human form. Had these poor men been put into a pen with bears and panthers they could not have been much more inhumanly and shockingly maimed.*

The cover of *Solano Republican* newspaper editor David Weir's 1957 book *That Fabulous Captain Waterman. Public domain.*

Waterman was called a "vile monster," a "disgrace" and a "bloody murderer," and it was said that if the charges against him were proven true, he should be burned alive.

On November 1, 1851, Captain Waterman and his mates were charged with "brutal and inhuman treatment of the ship's crew" and later stood trial. Waterman was convicted by a jury of beating one sick crewman, but the judge did not sentence him to any punishment. Douglass was convicted of murder for hitting a crewman in the head with a belaying pin (used to secure the rigging), but again no sentence is recorded in the historical record. Patterson was charged with kicking a crewman, resulting in his emasculation. He was found guilty and fined $50 (over $2,000 in 2025).

While the crew of *The Challenger* for the most part did not receive what might be considered justice for what transpired on their journey, the trials did have a lasting effect. These were the first "hell ship" trials and made possible the right of merchant sailors to seek relief in the courts and resulted in the Seaman's Act of 1915, which has been described as the Magna Carta of American sailors' rights.

Waterman retired and became a successful landlubbing farmer and then Fairfield's founding father.

1865: Murder in Cordelia

The book *The History of Solano County 1879* is a wonderful resource and includes a chapter titled "Murder Trials of Solano County." The one that best fits into this book's wheelhouse happened in Cordelia, once called Bridgeport, which the city of Fairfield annexed in 1971.

The *People v. Frank Grady* trial took place on September 6, 1865. A man identified in the book only by his surname, English, had two sons, Charles and Perry. Charles had a dustup with a fellow named Perry Durbin when he made a complaint to military officials at Benicia that Durbin and others were rejoicing over the assassination of President Abraham Lincoln.

Later, at a polling place in Bridgeport, Charles English and Durbin had words, and when Durbin made a motion as if drawing a weapon, Charles drew his revolver and commenced firing, hitting Durbin twice—in his left breast and his shoulder. Durbin then drew a knife and turned on Charles, who stumbled and fell while trying to escape. Durbin cut at his throat, which newspaper accounts described as "presenting a most horrible sight."

The elder English went to his son, and Durbin stabbed him three times, "making fearful wounds." Perry English tried to help his brother, but another man named Frank Grady shot and killed Perry. Although Grady took off on his horse, he was later captured and tried, but on September 19, 1866, he was acquitted.

1873: The Hanging of Pancho Valencia

On March 3, 1871, Joseph W. Hewitt from Pleasants Valley in Vacaville was killed. A few months before his murder, Hewitt had been in a quarrel with and killed a man named Parker Adams. He was tried and acquitted.

After that, a series of suspicious and seemingly malicious events happened to Hewitt. While he was crossing a bridge near his house, it collapsed (because some of the support logs had been sawed) and three of his horses that pulled on his team were killed. Next, his barn was set on fire. Then on March 3, 1871, two men came to his door at night and demanded entry. Hewitt didn't like their appearance and refused. One of then shot him in the chest, killing him.

Pancho Valencia had been a friend of Parker Adams, and while there was no evidence he was behind the bridge and barn incidents, he and his brother Guadalupe were arrested for the murder of Hewitt because they fit the description and were in the vicinity. Pancho Valencia came from a wealthy family but from all accounts was the black sheep and had served two previous stints in state prison. He and Guadalupe were tried and convicted, mainly based on the evidence presented by two of Hewitt's daughters.

Because of mistakes by the prosecution, an appeal was successful, and a new trial was ordered. Charges against Guadalupe, who was determined to be of a "very harmless and inoffensive disposition," were dismissed. A bit of a kerfuffle arose when court officers tried to explain to Guadalupe that he was free to go because he spoke almost no English and the interpreter had left the courtroom. Finally, someone suggested the word *vamoose* (in English, "let's go") and he was overcome with joy, so much so that he was trembling.

Pancho Valencia was convicted again, but that conviction was also overturned on another appeal. He was tried a third time in December 1872 and was convicted once and for all. He was sentenced to hang on January 31 of the following year.

Valencia appealed again but lost, and the governor refused to intervene. The gallows were built behind the Fairfield courthouse. They were shielded from public view by a wooden fence twenty feet high on three sides with the wall of the courthouse making the fourth.

The law at the time provided that executions had to be carried out privately and that no fewer than twelve respectable witnesses, selected by the sheriff, could be present. The sheriff sent out, for lack of a better description, execution invitations and almost immediately had twenty local men RSVP.

SHERIFF'S OFFICE,
SOLANO COUNTY.
FAIRFIELD......187..
To..............................
You are respectfully requested to be present at the County Jail to witness the execution of .... on the....day of..........187.., at ....o'clock....M.
....
Sheriff Solano County.
(Present this to the Jailor.)

The Solano County Sheriff's "execution invitation." *Fairfield Civic Center Library microfilm.*

The powers that be who were about to take his life tried repeatedly to get Pancho Valencia to confess, but he refused and claimed, as he always had, that he was innocent.

The morning of the execution, several people remarked that it was "just the day for a hanging." It was cold and gloomy with a thick mist that developed into drizzling rain. The designated hanging spot was filled with men who were both eager to witness the execution and a little ashamed of their own macabre curiosity. Many had set their watches in sync with the sheriff's so they would know the precise time of the execution.

When Valencia was brought out, he was offered one last chance to confess his crime but held to his claim of innocence.

There was a driving rain by that time, and it being Fairfield, wind gusts shook the boards that shielded the government work of death from the view of the uninvited.

Valencia was then placed on the drop, his face covered with a handkerchief, and a black silk cap was drawn over his head. Straps were buckled around his knees and ankles, his wrists were firmly strapped to his sides and his arms were tied behind him. The noose was adjusted, and at a signal from the sheriff, a deputy who had tears streaming down his face turned his head and used a penknife to cut the cord holding the drop in place.

A newspaper account of the moment of death read: "The drop fell and all that was mortal of Pancho Valencia dangled in the air."

At first it appeared as if death was instantaneous, but soon the body began to writhe and twitch as if attempting to break the straps that bound it. The spasmodic muscular movements went on for several seconds before Valencia was still.

After the body had been hanging for thirty minutes, all respect for the solemn scene appeared to be lost, and a buzz of conversation sprang up under the scaffold. Newspaper reports said that "the village wits began to pass jokes to and fro while they chatted and laughed as if a baseball match had just been finished."

The execution was only the second in Solano County. The first had taken place in Benicia in 1856, when it was the county seat during vigilante times. Beverly Wells (a man despite his "a boy named Sue" first name) was executed after being convicted of murder under "peculiarly atrocious circumstances."

A reporter attempted a wrap-up paragraph of the Pancho Valencia affair.

> *Thus has ended an episode in the history of Solano County which has involved the loss of lives and a large amount of the county's revenue ($30,000 to $40,000), to say nothing of the suffering entailed upon the living.*

But that wasn't the end.

Almost immediately, speculation arose about whether the local government had hanged an innocent man. Part of the reason was Valencia's assertion of his innocence even when standing on the drop ready to meet his maker. But there were other factors. According to the *San Francisco Chronicle*, he was "poorly defended in his last trial and his counsel was reported to have been drunk a portion of the time. The convicting testimony came from the daughter and wife of the murdered man and only one was able to say she was certain."

Public opinion was almost equally divided regarding Valencia's guilt or innocence.

Pancho Valencia is buried in the Saint Alphonsus Catholic Cemetery on Union Avenue and is the first person listed as being interred there.

1887: MIKE KEEFE CHEATS THE EXECUTIONER

On April 15, 1887, Mike Keefe was sentenced to be hanged for killing his wife. He had shot her once in the back and then emptied the rest of the contents of his revolver into her prostrate body.

Years before, Keefe had shot and killed a man near Folsom in a dispute about a gold mine claim and was sent to San Quentin State Prison for eleven years. He was pardoned after serving just two.

The gallows in Fairfield were built, and all was set for Keefe's day to meet the executioner, but instead of meeting him, he cheated him. The day before he was to have his life extinguished, Keefe stabbed himself on each side of his neck, severing the jugular vein. He also cut around one of his wrists.

Keefe lay in his cell covered up with his clothes trying to conceal the wounds. When they were discovered, Keefe fought the doctors who tried to sew up the wounds so he could be properly and officially killed the following day. Their efforts were in vain, as Keefe died later that afternoon.

An inquest was held, and Keefe's suicide was attributable to the negligence of the jail staff. Now, there are degrees of negligence, but what happened in the Keefe case just may be the granddaddy of them all. Keefe had been allowed to keep in his possession—while in jail, mind you—not one, but two knives for months *with the promise that he would not attempt to harm himself.*

A pre-1919 postcard of the Solano County Jail. *Public domain.*

But it was even worse.

That's because the knife that Keefe used to end his life was neither of those (so at least he kept his word) but a third one that he was able to obtain. It was also later revealed that another inmate had loaned him a whetstone to sharpen his blades.

A jail staff member went on record with the local newspaper as saying that the jail's discipline was very lax. The staff person's name and rank were not mentioned, but a good guess is that it was Captain Obvious.

1895: MONTALBANO MAKING MONEY

Counterfeiting was a huge problem on the Pacific coast. More manufacturers of phony coins were busted between 1885 and 1895 on the Pacific coast than in all other parts of the country combined. When it came to nineteenth-century counterfeiters, no one could touch Giavanno Montelbano. How big was he? Well, according to a February 24, 1895 *San Francisco Examiner* article, he "made and circulated more dangerous counterfeits of silver dollars, dimes and quarters in the past five years than any other ten operators combined."

It wasn't just quantity that set him apart from his counterfeiting peers either. His craftsmanship was unparalleled, and it took the most seasoned and professional eye to tell the difference between his fugazi coins and the real deal. Bankers were regularly snookered by his creations.

Montelbano was originally from Sicily, and his illegal mint was in a cave four miles from Fairfield in a lonely spot in the rugged foothills. The entrance was camouflaged so expertly that it was completely undetectable to the naked eye. He did his work in the subterranean counterfeit shop by candlelight at night and was only disturbed by the howls of coyotes or other wild animals.

Montalbano was meticulous about keeping his illicit workplace secret. He always removed his shoes before entering or exiting so as not to leave any telltale footprints outside. He buried the ashes for his furnace miles away from his shop.

It was only a freak accident that got him caught. A hunter fired a shot in the vicinity of Montalbano's counterfeiting cave, and it startled him so much that he evidently forgot himself and lifted the sod covering to have a look-see. Seeing some man coming out of nowhere as if from the bowels of the earth itself completely freaked out the hunter, who hightailed it outta there,

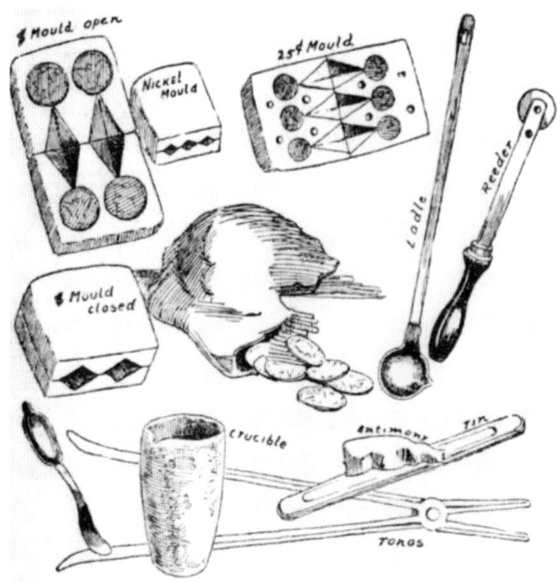

An 1875 illustration featuring some of Giavanno Montalbano's counterfeiting tools. *Newspapers.com.*

thinking Montalbano was a maniac or wild man. When the hunter came back with the authorities, Montalbano was discovered not to be a wild man but a con man who quickly became a jailed man.

1903: Jailbreak Foiled

On January 5, 1903, deputies at the Fairfield jail prevented a jailbreak on the last night of Sheriff Savage's term. Sam Heney, a "negro" (newspapers were big on highlighting race and national origin in those days) who was serving a sixty-day sentence for petty larceny, and two Greeks (see?) accused of participating in a riot in Benicia attempted to escape. For two days, they worked at cutting a hole in the roof of their cell.

Officers had been tipped off the day before the escape attempt, so evidently the jailhouse phrase "snitches get stitches" hadn't yet been coined in 1903. At eleven o'clock, Heney crawled through the hole in the roof and was immediately shot in the left arm by Deputy W.R. Reeves (no race or national origin was given, so that means he was white). The other prisoners quickly retired to their bunks and professed ignorance of the entire affair. The wounded would-be escapee was taken to the county hospital and had to have his arm amputated above the elbow.

2
PROMINENT FAIRFIELD CRIME STORIES, PART 1

Crime is a fact of the human species, a fact of that species alone, but it is above all the secret aspect, impenetrable and hidden. Crime hides, and by far the most terrifying things are those which elude us.
—Georges Bataille

The following stories, presented chronologically in two parts, are a representative sample of true crime stories that took place or were tried in Fairfield. Some are well-known and others are relatively obscure, but as each unfolded in daily life it captured the attention of locals, usually via the newspaper. Before reading on, be aware that some of the details are not for the squeamish.

1928: The Fairfield Chinatown Massacre

In 1999, Fairfield-based candy company Jelly Belly, in conjunction with a casino, created a jar ten feet tall that contained 2,160,000 jellybeans. Then in 2010, the confectioners crafted a thirty-nine-foot-long art piece for the World Expo that used approximately 617,000 jellybeans. For both efforts, Jelly Belly was enshrined in the pages of the vaunted Guinness Book of Records.

Those whimsical records are what the city touts and make residents proud. A state record that Fairfield set in 1928, however, was a very different kind.

No locals' chests swelled with pride for the record set that year. It was for the most victims of a mass murderer in California.

The vicious and unthinkable crimes took place on August 21, 1928, at the Hatch Ranch in the Suisun Valley. A Chinatown had bloomed in Rockville near Suisun Creek, where descendants of the first Chinese immigrants, lured to California by the 1849 gold rush, settled.

The first calls for help came into the sheriff's office at around 9:00 a.m., and it was reported that a Chinese gunman had killed a couple of men. When Sheriff Jack Thornton and two deputies arrived at the scene, it was far grislier than they could have imagined.

It was not a whodunit. The killer was named immediately as Leung Ying. He was described in period newspaper accounts as having a badly pockmarked face and had the unusual habit of walking on his toes like a cat.

Wholesale Killer

Leung Ying, Chinese, was arrested in a chicken house at Grass Valley, Cal., by officers who said he confessed to the killing of 10 of his countrymen with a hatchet and rifle and seriously wounding several others near Fairfield.

Fairfield mass murderer Leung Ying in 1928. *Fairfield Civic Center Library microfilm.*

As often happens in the rear-view mirror of a murder, the killer is described differently by different people. Some of his peers, who were evidently hedonists, said that Ying was well-liked and was a swell guy. They said he dispensed liquor, was a narcotics user and dealer and even brought "easy" women to the ranches on payday. But the majority told disturbing tales about him boasting about having previously killed three men, which he signified by three notches on his gun.

Newspapers, as they are sometimes wont to do, hyped up the horror, and the murder scene was described as "a wild orgy of butchering and shooting." The facts are as follows: While high on cocaine, Leung Ying took a rifle and shot his boss Wong Gee, who was smoking an opium pipe before work in a secret underground room. Another worker, Chan Yin, was shot there as well.

To make it worse, Ying used homemade so-called Dum Dum bullets, which are hollow points that expand and cause much more damage than a normal bullet.

Ying then found Wong's brother Wong Hing Chong and shot him. He also fatally wounded Wah Way, a cook.

Then Ying walked two hundred yards to Wong Gee's home. On the way, he shot Yeung Soon, who was sorting pears. Once he got to the house, Ying shot Wong Gee's fifteen-year-old daughter, Nellie, in the abdomen. She held on to life for five days after the initial killing spree but ultimately became the final victim of Ying's murderous rampage.

Wong Gee's wife was carrying her ten-day-old baby, who had not yet been named. Ying shot the woman through the heart as she tried desperately to shield her child.

Next, he went to a crib and shot three-year-old Johnny Gee through the heart and crushed his head with a hatchet.

Low Chuck, the camp cook, was the next victim. He was shot through the stomach and died later at the county hospital.

Evidently, Leung Ying ran out of ammunition, because he retrieved a cleaver from the kitchen. After splitting the head of four-year-old Willie Wong, he returned to Mrs. Wong Gee, moved her lifeless body and severed the baby's throat from ear to ear.

The only members of Wong Gee's family left alive were seven-year-old Ruthie and nine-year-old Helen, who were hiding upstairs.

A witness said that after Ying finished his bloodthirsty work, he stopped by a cutting shed where other laborers were cutting pears. He ate a pear or two, threaten to kill them all and took off into the orchard.

Leung Ying jumped into his Dodge roadster and escaped to Grass Valley, where his brother lived. Later that day, the police found him in a chicken house holding an empty rifle, and although he resisted, they arrested him there. Ying readily confessed his crimes and soon was brought back to Fairfield. Word spread about the atrocities he had committed, and large crowds gathered at Nevada City and other places along the route to Solano County's seat to get a glance at the murderer.

The story of the drug-fueled massacre became nationwide news. When caught, Ying said the reason for the murders was that others in the village were plotting to kill him by poisoning his food.

A different reason was proposed in a 1981 interview with Evelyn Lockie published in the December 1985 issue of the *Solano Historian* magazine. Lockie, who grew up in the area and knew Wong Gee, covered the story as a Fairfield correspondent for *The Sacramento Bee*:

> *As far as we could find out, and according to his own version, he had been the subject of much teasing. He was an ugly little man, whose face was deeply pock-marked, probably from smallpox, and he wasn't*

> *too bright. The teasing irritated him. He found out that opium swept away his unhappiness and became addicted to it. As "hopheads" were not encouraged on this ranch, he couldn't get any opium, and this coupled with his being teased so much led his warped mind to the path of murder. He knew exactly who his targets would be and methodically went about disposing of them.*

Yet another theory was that the murders were part of a tong war. Tongs were secret societies or sworn brotherhoods that often provided services such as immigrant counseling, Chinese schools and English classes for adults for Chinatown communities. They also were sometimes tied to organized criminal activity.

When the sheriffs investigated the murders, they disarmed all the Chinese residents to prevent a possible tong flare up. Several rifles, shotguns, pistols and knives were found, along with opium pipes.

Left, Solano County Sheriff J.R. Thornton; *center*, Nevada County Sheriff George Carter; *right*, Solano County Deputy Sheriff George N. Fraser; *front*, Fairfield killer Leung Ying. *Newspapers.com*

There were more than one hundred Chinese residents who were present at the Fairfield jail when Ying was brought there. County and state officers were heavily armed and on guard for any trouble. Members of the Bing Kong and the Hop Sing tongs were present, but neither saw it as a tong matter.

They told the sheriff's office that they wanted to see if they had captured the right man so they could sleep assured it was Ying. They said that if he should escape the white authorities, the tong would take up the trail for weeks, months and even years if necessary to get their man.

While there were many theories of what would lead Ying to commit such atrocities, the most plausible motive was that three months earlier Ying had attempted an assault on Nellie Wong and Wong Gee ordered him to leave the ranch.

Once at the courthouse, Ying's arraignment had to be postponed from 10:00 a.m. until the afternoon because of the threatening crowd. One unidentified Chinese man made his way to the second floor of the building with a drawn revolver but was knocked down and disarmed by a deputy.

Ying had previously been charged with murder, not once, but twice. The first time was in San Francisco in 1923, and the second was during a tong war in Stockton the following year.

The funeral procession for the first ten victims was held the day before Nellie Wong died and brought the total to eleven.

Leung Ying was never remorseful and in fact asked to be released from his cell to kill a certain elderly Chinese woman, swearing he would return after her murder.

Ying tried to hang himself with a blanket the night after his arrest but was stopped by guards. He then spent the night banging his head against the floor and the walls while crying out for narcotics.

When his trial started, spectators were searched before entering the courtroom, and a Chinese man was discovered to have a steel bar stuck down his pants leg. Expert witnesses testified that Ying was sane, and his defense (the fear of being poisoned) was refuted. While his food had a lot of oil that might have made him sick, it was not lethal.

On August 31, 1928, Leung Ying pleaded guilty to the murders and was sentenced to death by hanging. When he was sentenced, he grinned and said through an interpreter, "I'm glad it's over."

The execution date was set for November 9, but Ying hanged himself with a bath towel on October 22 in his cell at San Quentin State Prison.

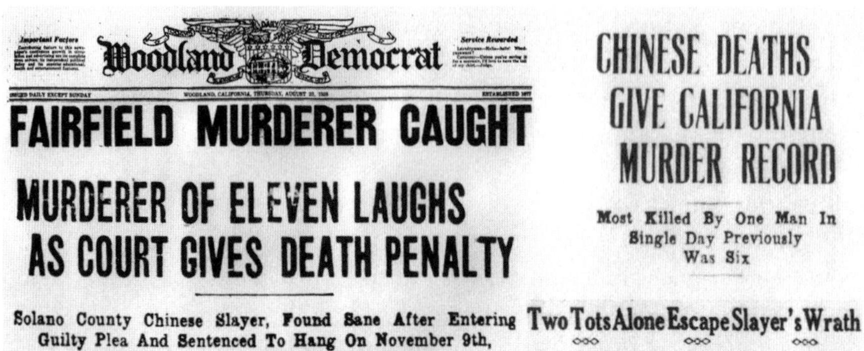
Woodland Democrat

FAIRFIELD MURDERER CAUGHT

MURDERER OF ELEVEN LAUGHS AS COURT GIVES DEATH PENALTY

Solano County Chinese Slayer, Found Sane After Entering Guilty Plea And Sentenced To Hang On November 9th, To-day Is In San Quentin Penitentiary

CHINESE DEATHS GIVE CALIFORNIA MURDER RECORD

Most Killed By One Man In Single Day Previously Was Six

Two Tots Alone Escape Slayer's Wrath

Little Girls' Flight Saves Them From Fate Of Others

Headlines about Fairfield mass murder Leung Ying. *Public domain.*

It was the first time in San Quentin' history that a condemned murderer cheated the gallows by suicide. The Fairfield newspaper, the *Solano Republican*, reported the suicide with its style of mixing editorial comment in with news reports. It said that by taking his own life, Ying "saved the state 15 feet of well-stretched hemp." It ended by saying that "Chinese in Suisun Valley were satisfied with the results of the bath towel party."

A sad postscript to the Ying story that could be filed in the Even Horrific Records Were Made to Be Broken Department is that just three months later Charles Braker from Santa Rosa killed sixteen people before taking his own life.

1929: Wayne Smith—The First Solano County Insanity Defense

Irma Sternberg was a well-liked 1923 graduate of Armijo High School and excelled on the tennis team there. After graduation, she moved in with her sister in Rio Vista, worked at a bank there and in 1927 was named the Isleton Asparagus Festival pageant queen.

Her long-term boyfriend was Wayne Smith, and their relationship, like many, had ups and downs. On January 29, 1929, it turned tragic.

Evidently, Wayne had tried for years to persuade Irma to become his bride. On that fateful evening, after picking her up, they drove around the block and stopped on a side street under the shade of some trees. Smith asked once again for her hand, and when Sternberg refused, he shot her twice and then shot himself. Sternberg was hit in the left lower abdomen, just above the groin and again on the left side in the abdomen. The lower shot carried a full length of corset steel into her vital organs.

The shot that Smith fired into himself entered his right side, followed the rib around the body and lodged near his spine.

Sternberg was taken to Sutter Hospital, where she died the next morning. Smith ultimately recovered from his wound.

When questioned by Sacramento County officers at Sutter Hospital, Smith made the following statement: "I went over to see Miss Sternberg. She came out of her apartment and sat in my coupe. We had an argument and she turned me down. I shot her twice in the abdomen with a .38 caliber revolver which I carry for personal protection. I have been keeping company with Miss Sternberg for about five years. I hope I die."

Wayne Smith was charged with murder, and the evidence, along with his fatalistic confession, seemed to make an airtight case. Smith owned up to his evil deed and was prepared to face the consequences for it.

But that was before defense attorneys got involved.

In April 1929, Smith had his preliminary hearing and entered two pleas to the charge of murder in the first degree: not guilty and not guilty by reason of insanity. The latter plea was the first time it had been entered into a case in the history of Solano County.

If Smith was found guilty of the crime, then it would be necessary to try him before the same jury as to whether he was sane at the time of the murder. If found sane, he would have to face the death sentence. If found insane, he could escape the most extreme penalty.

The trial began later that month, and through his attorney, Luke Howe, Smith recanted his admissions to the authorities and to at least six others of intentionally shooting Sternberg.

Most damaging were the dying words of Irma Sternberg to her sister, spoken at the hospital: "He pointed the gun at my heart and shot me twice."

The defense argued that a murder charge would have made sense if Smith had just recently bought a pistol to kill his girlfriend, but he had owned the weapon in question for two years. In fact, in 1927 he was going to kill himself, and Sternberger took the pistol away from him for two months.

On the night of the killing, Sternberger had found the gun in the car and tried to keep it away from Smith, the defense argued. Smith, despondent about Sternberger wanting to break up, grabbed for it to end his life and it went off twice and then he shot himself.

As for the incriminating statements that he made afterward to law enforcement officials and six other individuals, they were explained away as irrelevant because he was under the influence of pain and opiates and had no actual recollection of what had transpired.

Smith's lawyer evidently had a flair for the dramatic, and since Mother's Day had recently been celebrated, he quoted the lyrics of a sentimental song, "Mother of Mine," and said to the jury, "I thought what a wonderful gift lay in your power to give [Smith's] mother—the gift of her son's freedom and life."

Alleged Slayer

WAYNE SMITH, Rio Vista youth who is now on trial in the Solano County Superior Court on a charge of having slain his sweetheart, Miss Irma Sternberg of Rio Vista on the night of January 29th.

Wayne Smith, who killed his girlfriend Irma Sternberg in Rio Vista. *Fairfield Civic Center Library microfilm.*

He also used an example of a play where a boy witnesses a murder when drunk and took the blame for it when he actually had nothing to do with it.

District Attorney Brantley W. Dobbins was having none of it: "This is a serious case. A case of murder. We claim the killing of a young girl, 23 years of age. Shot and murdered in cold blood without an opportunity to save her life."

Dobbins compared the defendant's defense to the octopus in Victor Hugo's *Toilers of the Sea*. He said it was like the "devil fish" emitting a black fluid to cover its escape. The question about the gun was not how long Smith had owned it or what it had been used for previously but what he had done with it on January 29, 1929.

Dobbins said that the defective memory excuse for what happened that night was another ink cloud. He ridiculed the defense's argument that the worst thing the jury could find Smith guilty of was manslaughter, saying it was an admission of the weakness of their case.

Then Dobbins, who also had a flair for the dramatic, pointed to the graveyard where Sternberg was buried (which could be seen from the courtroom window) and said: "This young girl lying in yonder cemetery had a right to live. And the people of the state ask you in all sincerity, based upon the facts of the evidence, to bring in a verdict of murder in the first degree, without any recommendation for life imprisonment."

He finished up by quoting the Bible to the jury of ten men and two women: "Whosever sheddeth man's blood, by man shall his blood be shed."

The case was given to the jury at 2:30 p.m., and by 5:00 p.m., they had reached a verdict.

Guilty.

Of manslaughter.

The defense quickly made a motion to withdraw the second plea of not guilty by reason of insanity, but the judge denied it. Smith was later found to be sane.

The jury's deliberations on reaching the manslaughter verdict evidently were not secret because they were reported extensively at the time. They were similar to the plot of the play/movie *12 Angry Men*, in which a jury is swayed from one way of thinking to another over time. On the first ballot, the jurors were evenly divided on Smith's guilt or innocence. The second ballot was eight for manslaughter and four for murder. The third ballot was eleven for manslaughter and one for second-degree murder, and the fourth was the unanimous manslaughter verdict.

The manslaughter charge carried an indeterminate sentence of one to ten years. After a year in prison, the convicted individual would be given their sentence. Smith was sent to San Quentin State Prison and after a year was given the maximum of ten years. However, he applied for parole in 1931 and was released in 1933.

In the first insanity defense case in Solano County, some may deduce that, given the facts of the case, the only insane thing about it was a man killing a woman in cold blood and only doing four years in prison.

1929: The Murder of the "Mad Heiress" Edith Wolfskill

The huge headline of the August 28, 1903 *San Francisco Call* newspaper screamed "Demented Young Woman Escapes." The woman in question was then twenty-two-year-old Edith Irene Wolfskill. She had been sent to the California General Hospital in San Francisco because, according to newspaper accounts, her mind had become "wrecked from over-study."

Edith Wolfskill was reported to be suffering from "religious mania" and attracted crowds when she would kneel on crowded city sidewalks and pray.

She escaped from the hospital sometime in the night after being taken there, and once it was discovered that she was missing, an intensive search began.

After her escape from the mental hospital, her relatives hired the famous Pinkerton Detective Agency to help track her down. Forty-four hours later, Edith Wolfskill was discovered in Colma (about nine miles from San Francisco) at the bottom of a deep canyon, apparently kneeling in prayer. It took some doing to save her from the treacherously deep sides of the canyon, and she had to be forcibly put into a carriage, where she knelt on the floor of the vehicle the whole way home.

Edith Wolfskill was related to the wealthy Wolfskill family, which figured prominently in early California history. Her great-uncle John Wolfskill was the first English-speaking settler in Solano County. Miss Wolfskill and her brothers, Matthew and Ney Wolfskill, had inherited a fortune of $1.6 million (over $50 million in 2025) from their father when he died in 1913.

"The Mad Heiress" Edith Irene Wolfskill in 1903. *Fairfield Civic Center Library microfilm.*

Privacy laws about health issues and fear of litigation in the early twentieth century not being what they are today, Edith Wolfskill's mental problems were reported in newspaper stories alongside other facts. And sometimes they were not kind.

In addition to the aforementioned term *demented*, she was also referred to as "mentally unbalanced," "eccentric," "peculiar" and even "the mad heiress."

Because of her mental state, Edith Wolfskill was in the alternate custody of her two brothers. Nurses took care of her physical needs, and the Los Angeles Trust Company took care of her considerable estate.

Twenty-six years later, on July 14, 1929, Edith Irene Wolfskill went missing again.

She had moved from Los Angeles to Mankas Corner in Fairfield two years earlier, and she went for a morning walk at around 7:30 a.m. wearing a blue gingham dress. At 11:30 a.m., when lunch was about to be served, Wolfskill was nowhere to be found.

Left, Edith Irene Wolfskill and her brothers, Matthew (*top*) and Ney Wolfskill. *Fairfield Civic Center Library microfilm.*

Solano County Sheriff John R. Thornton, assisted by a twenty-two-man posse, volunteers and Wolfskill's brothers, scoured the countryside around Fairfield. They followed the footprints from the high-heeled shoes she was wearing until they lost the trail. Aerial searches were performed in a plane, police dogs were used and divers searched for her body in Curry Lake (the source of Vallejo's water supply at that time).

Weeks went by, and besides random footprints found in Gordon Valley, the searchers turned up nothing. Theories of what had happened to Wolfskill ranged from her being kidnapped to being killed by itinerant farmworkers. A reward of $5,000 was offered for her discovery, dead or alive.

Newspapers all over the country covered the details of the story as it unfolded.

A July 22 newspaper account featured Betty Ritschard, Edith Wolfskill's former nurse, telling authorities she was convinced Miss Wolfskill had hidden in a ravine on her own ranch and died from exposure. She explained that she would have done that to hide from Mrs. J.E. Conklin, her new nurse, who went on duty the very day Wolfskill disappeared.

It turned out the former nurse's speculation was very close to what actually happened.

Around five o'clock on September 19, 1929, eighteen-year-old Bernold Glashoff, son of rancher Hermann Glashoff, discovered the badly decomposed body of Edith Irene Wolfskill in a creek in Wooden Valley on the Williams ranch. She was face down and clothed in brown men's carpenter's overalls and a flannel shirt.

While the mystery of her location was finally solved, another mystery began. The spot where she had been discovered was a mile and a half from the Wolfskill ranch and had been searched repeatedly.

After examination, Wolfskill's body showed evidence of having long been dead and of lying face downward in the same spot. Grass was growing through her hair, and her back had been exposed to excessive heat or sunlight.

Bernold Glashoff pointing to the circled area where he found the body of Edith Irene Wolfskill. *Fairfield Civic Center Library microfilm.*

There was no evidence of injury to any of her bones and none of her being poisoned.

An inquest was held at the Solano County Courthouse, and the witnesses included Bernold Glashoff, undersheriff Charles F. Perry, undertaker Arnold Maupin, Ney Wolfskill, Nelda Wolfskill (a niece who identified the remains) and Dr. Andrew Finan, who conducted the first autopsy.

Several things pointed to foul play. The spot where Wolfskill was found, as already stated, had been searched repeatedly, for one thing. That her clothes had been changed was another. Those who knew Edith best were aware that she had a phobia about even touching other people's clothes. The shoes that were next to her body were like new and unscuffed. If she had been rambling around the hills for weeks, how had her shoes remained so pristine?

But assumptions are not proof, and after the witnesses testified and doctors read their findings, a coroner's jury closed the sad case of Edith Irene Wolfskill with four words: "death from causes unknown."

Bernold Glashoff eventually had to sue to receive the $5,000 reward for finding Wolfskill. The bank initially refused payment because Glashoff had accidentally discovered the body and did not know who she was.

Wolfskill's brothers, who had not spoken to each other in twenty years, predictably fought each other in court over their deceased sibling's $800,000 (over $11 million in 2025) estate.

The *San Francisco Chronicle* labeled the whole Edith Wolfskill spectacle as "one of the most baffling cases in Northern California."

1931: THE CASE OF THE HEADLESS HINDU

Sant Ram Pande, who was beheaded and dubbed the "Headless Hindu" in newspaper accounts. *Fairfield Civic Center Library microfilm.*

By 1931, a startling number of Hindu men in the United States had turned up dead, with the number somewhere between eighteen and twenty-two. Sant Ram Pande, a thirty-two-year-old Hindu language interpreter for the Sacramento Police Department and University of California Berkeley student, paused his educational career to focus on the murders and work with the authorities to find a resolution.

Pande soon became a victim himself and the best known.

On March 4, 1931, Pande's headless body was discovered anchored by a seventy-five-pound tractor wheel in Cache Slough near Rio Vista. The only reason his body was identifiable was that he had feared he would be killed and asked the chief of the State Bureau of Criminal Identification, Clarence S. Morrill, to record his fingerprints. He also kept a diary, which furnished valuable information to investigators.

Pande was a follower of civil rights pioneer Mahatma Gandhi in the Indian Nationalist movement. While he followed many of Gandhi's teachings, evidently, he did not adhere to the Indian leader's nonviolence philosophy. The Berkeley chief of police confirmed that as a precaution Pande had been granted permission to carry firearms.

Pande was the second Sacramento Police Department Indian interpreter to be slain. The previous one, Rham Dhami, was shot to death in Sacramento in February 1931. Several Hindus were rounded up and questioned about Pande's murder, but eventually the "Headless Hindu" case was considered unsolved and listed as a homicide by unknown persons.

The Hindu kidnappings, disappearances and murders continued. The working theory of the cases was that there was an illegal smuggling ring that brought Hindus into the country for a price, and when someone got mouthy about it, they would be killed. Local authorities could get only so far in their investigations before they were hit with a wall of silence when witnesses realized it would cost them their lives and refused to testify.

Hindu murder suspect Lachman Singh. *Fairfield Civic Center Library microfilm.*

A 1931 editorial by a Hindu writer pointedly charged that the so-called Headless Hindu case, one of dozens known to law enforcement, was the first to be thoroughly investigated. It is not easy to glean motives when it comes to how law enforcement agencies from the past prioritized the use of prosecutorial resources. It is easy, however, to find anti-Hindu articles in old newspapers. As far back as 1910, a front-page article in the *Vacaville Reporter* lamented that "HINDUS ARE SWARMING IN" with the subheader "They are the most objectionable of all Asiatics."

In 1933, Lachman Singh, who had been questioned and released in the murder of Pande, was taken into custody and charged with a different murder. Singh was accused of killing Dhurm Singh on Ryer Island in the Sacramento River. Dhurm Singh was seen as the mastermind of Ghadar, a Hindu political party. Lachman Singh, no relation to Dhurm but actually an uncle of Sant Ram Pande, was arraigned in Fairfield in June 1933.

As they prepared to finally bring someone to justice, the authorities were thwarted yet again. This time, it was not by the sudden silence of witnesses but something much more dramatic. Lachman Singh took his own life by removing his turban and using the wrapping to hang himself from a bar at the top of his cell.

A rather macabre postscript to the Headless Hindu case is that in 1960, Solano County Deputy Sheriff Lawrence Madsen posed for a picture in the *Vallejo News Chronicle* with mementoes collected from celebrated cases. The display case was at the county jail in Fairfield, and in the picture Madsen points to the turban with which Lachman Singh hanged himself.

Also among the items are ten jars containing the preserved fingers of Sant Ram Pande, which had been removed for identification.

Deputy Sheriff Lawrence Madsen indicates the turban with which a Hindu Priest hanged himself in the county jail in Fairfield after decapitating a Stockton man and throwing his body in the Sacramento River. The turban is one of scores of items associated with celebrated police cases, on display in the branch sheriff's office at 1350 Virginia St. Immediately below the turban are 10 jars containing the fingers of the priest's victim.—News-Chronicle Photo.

A 1960 photo of a Deputy Sheriff with Lachman Singh's turban, with which he hanged himself, and jars containing the Headless Hindu's fingers. The caption is incorrect, as Lachman Singh was not found to have been Sant Ram Pande's killer. *Fairfield Civic Center Library microfilm.*

1944: MADELINE CHADBOURNE AND THE BIRTHDAY DEATHDAY

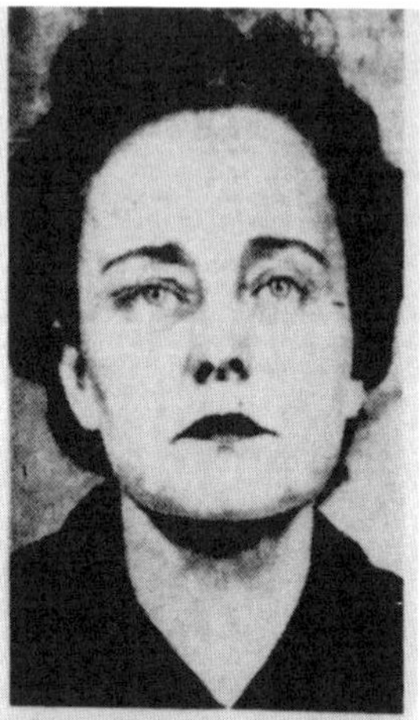

At noon on October 18, 1944, Warner Chadbourne, prominent Suisun Valley resident and member of a pioneering Solano County family, was serenaded by his fellow members of the Fairfield Lions Club for his fiftieth birthday. He had no way of knowing then that his birthday would also be his deathday.

That evening, Warner's wife, forty-six-year-old Madeline Chadbourne, shot him dead and then tried to kill herself.

Solano County Undersheriff Ernest Lockie and Deputy Sheriff Jule Pritchard arrived at the Chadbourne home to find the decedent's brother, Grant; with his wife, Grace; and well-known local physician Dr. Gordon Bunney already there. Madeline Chadbourne was lying on the couch being treated by Dr. Bunney, and Warner's body was in an adjoining bedroom. The bullet Madeline had shot herself with entered her left breast but was deflected by a rib so she had only a severe flesh wound.

Mrs. Madeline Chadbourne, who is charged with the murder of her husband, Warner S. Chadbourne, in their Suisun Valley ranch home near Fairfield on the night of October 18th. Mrs. Chadbourne, who shot herself in the breast, was transferred from a hospital to the Solano County Jail Friday. She was arraigned yesterday.

Madeleine Chadbourne, who shot and killed her husband, Warner; she then shot herself but lived. *Fairfield Civic Center Library microfilm.*

The Chadbournes were well-known in Solano and Napa Counties. Madeline Chadbourne was the daughter of a former Napa mayor. She had worked as a Solano County law librarian and was the secretary to a Superior Court judge.

Warner Chadbourne was a Suisun City rancher and superintendent of the Lambert Marketing Company, a fruit packing concern. He was also an accomplished photographer who had received national recognition for his work and belonged to numerous local civic organizations.

On the surface, the Chadbournes were living the dream, but behind closed doors it was a completely different story.

There had been ongoing issues with Warner's excessive drinking and infidelity, specifically with two women from Lake County and one from Ukiah. That evening, the couple argued about Warner's attentions to the women in question, and he angrily announced he was going to go and rejoin his Lake County mini-harem. It was then that Madeline went into another room and got Warner's .44-caliber revolver and fired one shot into his head, instantly killing him.

Madeline's twenty-three-year-old daughter from a previous marriage, Drussela, was at a USO dance that evening but returned later that night.

Family issues in the Chadbourne clan evidently went beyond Warner's married life. His mother, Edith Chadbourne, had died on October 7, 1944, and left most of her $7,000 estate (about $90,000 in 2025) to Warner. For reasons not made clear in historical documents, Warner's only brother, Grant Chadbourne, was left exactly $1.

Ouch.

On November 27, 1944, Madeline Chadbourne was indicted by the Solano County grand jury and charged with murder. The following month, she entered a plea of not guilty and not guilty by reason of insanity.

Madeline Chadbourne (*left*) and her daughter Drussela Chadbourne. *Newspapers.com.*

Because of Madeline's ties with local judges and other officers of the court, they all had to recuse themselves. Consequently, Judge W.T. Belieu from Glenn County presided over the trial, and the Monterey County district attorney, Anthony Brazil, was brought in to try the case. The trial started in January 1945, and Brazil stated at the outset that "Mrs. Chadbourne has no defense whatever," as "she deliberately premeditated and killed her husband who never knew what hit him." He asked the jury to bring in a verdict of guilty of first-degree murder.

Madeline's defense attorney, A.G. Bailey, insisted that his client shot her husband in self-defense, as she feared violence at his hand.

Brazil came out swinging in the trial. He called Deputy Sheriff Jule Pritchard and Grace Chadbourne, Grant's wife, to the stand. Pritchard testified that once he arrived at her home, Madeleine admitted to him that she had shot Warner. Then later, when she had been taken to the Bunney Hospital on Empire Street, he reported she said, "I never thought I would be classed as a murderer. I am."

Details about the argument and aftermath were revealed in open court by Pritchard. He said that Madeline told him the two Lake County women called Warner to congratulate him on his fiftieth birthday. Madeline accused him of being too intimate with them. Warner started to get dressed to visit his female friends and said, "You don't take as good care of me as they do. I'm through with you. I want a divorce and this time I mean it. I'm through with you for good—you dirty little slut!"

Madeline then said she was going to accompany him, and he replied, "The hell you are. I'm going alone and I'm going for good." She went and got the gun and, when she stepped back into the bedroom, said, "You're going on a trip, all right. But we are both going together."

Grace Chadbourne testified that she overheard a conversation between Madeline and her daughter, Drussela, in which the accused said: "Honey, your mother is a murderer. I guess I'll get the gas chamber."

Dr. Gordon Bunney also testified and explained matter-of-factly what he experienced the night of the incident. He also revealed that while he was there, he had been presented with a pivotal piece of evidence for the defense: a holographic (handwritten) will by Madeline Chadbourne. It was written on the back of a sheet of blank checks and was inside an envelope addressed to Madeline's daughter, Drussela.

The will was dated October 7, 1944, the day that Edith Chadbourne had died. It purported to show that Madeline had feared for her life at least eleven days before she killed Warner. In it, Madeline left her entire

Madeline Chadbourne crying while testifying in her murder trial. *Fairfield Civic Center Library microfilm.*

estate to Drussela. The will stated: "I am taking this precaution to protect her since Warner is so very drunk tonight, although his mother has just passed away. He has threatened to shoot me and probably will not, but I must think of Drussela."

The document was signed "Madeline Chadbourne, written in hurry."

Once the prosecution rested, Madeline took the stand and told of the abuse she suffered in her fourteen-year marriage to Warner, which she called "a living hell." She wept frequently and looked frail, as she had lost twelve pounds since October and probably weighed only about one hundred pounds. Still, she held her own under withering cross-examination by Brazil.

As the trial progressed, each day more and more spectators were turned away from the packed courtroom. It was said that the trial turned neighbor against neighbor depending on whether they believed Madeline had acted due to self-preservation or with maliciousness. The looming shadow of the gas chamber hung over the proceedings and could seem closer or farther away depending on which side scored points on any given day.

Particularly damning testimony came from Kenneth Finch, Warner's business partner. Finch described his slain colleague as his best friend and yet testified to several times when Warner drunkenly threatened to kill Madeline or Mattie, as he called her.

Drussela testified to Warner's drinking and abuse and to two separate times he threatened her mother. On one of them, she testified that Warner said, "If she won't give me a divorce, I'll get rid of her one way or the other."

Warner's excessive drinking was well established by defense witnesses and even conceded by those for the prosecution. His cousin Joe Chadbourne, who was a music teacher at Armijo High School, testified that from time to time he would be called upon to come over to calm an inebriated and angry Warner by playing Tchaikovsky or other classical music.

Drussela and Madeline Chadbourne shortly after Madeline was acquitted of murdering her husband. *Fairfield Civic Center Library microfilm.*

Still, both sides agreed that on the night he was killed, Warner Chadbourne was completely sober. To Madeline, that made it even worse, as his rage was not fueled by alcohol, just internal fury.

In his closing argument, Special Prosecutor Brazil said, "The state will contend that the evidence heretofore advanced serves to warrant the asking of First Degree Murder without recommendation for clemency."

In other words, the death penalty.

The defense pointed out that Madeline Chadbourne had married Warner after he had lost everything during the Great Depression and helped rebuild their wealth in many ways, even by laboring in the fruit harvest. She loved him, and all was well until his drinking escalated and he fell in love with his extramarital fling. Bailey said Madeline shot her husband when he lunged at her and threatened her with violence.

"She did what anyone else would do: she shot in self-defense."

The jury was given their instructions by the judge and began their deliberations on February 1, 1945. Five hours later, the six men and six women of the jury delivered ten words: "We, the jury find the defendant, Madeline Chadbourne, not guilty."

Madeline Chadbourne embraced her lawyer and daughter. Brazil looked amazed, shrugged and called the verdict "a rank miscarriage of justice."

Since she was acquitted, Madeline Chadbourne automatically inherited two estates. The first was Warner's, and the second was Edith

Chadbourne's, as she was the sole heir. Had she been convicted, Grant Chadbourne would have received the estate of Edith Chadbourne and one-half of Warner's estate.

Madeline Chadbourne died in 1977.

In 1947, Drussela Chadbourne married her Armijo Class of 1939 classmate Manuel Campos, who owned several Food Fair supermarkets, was a local politician and two-term mayor and is now the namesake of a parkway in Fairfield. They were married for forty-eight years and had three children. Drussela died in 1995.

1950: ROBERT HORNBUCKLE—THE CLAW HAMMER KILLER

The initial sparks of infatuation that can lead to the roaring fire of love can originate anywhere. But for the flames to last, having them start when both of the parties are in jail is probably not the most ideal scenario. That is where twenty-seven-year-old Robert Hornbuckle met twenty-five-year-old Cheryl Jean Davis in 1950. He was serving a jail sentence in Woodland, California, for an assault and battery charge against his wife. Davis was locked in an adjoining cell in the women's section for drunk driving and driving without a license.

Their romance began with the pair talking to each other through the wall. When Hornbuckle was released, he put up the bail for Davis, and after his divorce was finalized, they began living together in Sacramento. During their cohabitation, Davis drank heavily and the jailbirds-turned-lovebirds had a series of violent quarrels.

On the Wednesday before Thanksgiving, the couple were driving from Sacramento to Woodland in Hornbuckle's convertible coupe and drinking. According to Hornbuckle, they argued about money and whiskey, and Davis accused him of being unfaithful to her. She slapped him, pushed her foot against his on the gas pedal, grabbed the steering wheel and threatened to crash the car.

Hornbuckle pulled the car over beside the highway, calmly took a claw hammer from a toolbox in the back seat and proceeded to hit Davis in the head with it "more times than I could count."

The Solano County Coroner's Office did count and said Davis had been struck nine times on the head. Her skull was fractured from ear to ear, and a hole was poked through one temple.

Hornbuckle stuffed Davis's body in the trunk and drove back to their Sacramento apartment. He changed his bloody clothes and brought a blanket to cover the bloody front passenger seat. Overcome with grief for his impulsive act of murder, Hornbuckle decided to end it all by driving to San Francisco to jump off the Golden Gate Bridge. But on the way, a tire blew out right before he made it to Fairfield.

Robert Hornbuckle, the Claw Hammer Killer. *Newspapers.com.*

He then thumbed for a ride, and a car stopped to pick him up. It was a California Highway patrolman (!) who took him to Fairfield. There Hornbuckle took a bus to San Francisco. On the way, he changed his mind about suicide and the next day called the police and told them about the dead woman in the trunk of his car. Once the call came in, the car was located by the very same California Highway patrolman who had given Hornbuckle a ride the day before.

Then Chief Criminal Deputy Sheriff Stanley Emerson of the Solano County Sheriff's Office had just sat down to Thanksgiving dinner when he got the call about the case. He spoke about it in a 2019 interview:

> *The interesting part of that whole damn thing was where to try the case? You charge them where the person died and it was near a county line so there was debate about whether it should be Yolo, Sacramento or Solano County....I walked every place where there was a levee road looking for a place where it could have occurred and I found the spot where there was drag marks. I also found a single earring that matched one in the trunk, so Solano County tried him.*

In February 1951, Robert Hornbuckle was sentenced to life in prison.

1952: The Freudenbergs—Booze, Bickering, Buicks and Bullets

On October 18, 1952, Elizabeth Anne Freudenberg, thirty-two, was fatally wounded while she and her husband, Herman Lee Freudenberg Jr., thirty-nine, struggled over a gun in their Fairfield home.

The story dominated both the local and regional news for over a year, as it involved a prominent local couple. Herman was a successful banker and car dealer who owned Freudenberg Buick at 1246 Texas Street (the building is still there in 2025 and was used for years as the circulation building for the *Daily Republic*). His father and namesake started a car dealership in Vallejo in 1912 and actually sold the first Buick in the state of California.

Elizabeth Anne Freudenberg, known as Bette to her friends, is described in newspaper accounts as a pretty socialite wife who had three children, two of them from a previous marriage. In the 1950 U.S. census, her occupation was listed as "keeping house." Her father, Glenn Stanley, like her husband's dad, was a prominent Vallejo businessman.

The Freudenbergs had been active in local social and civic circles since they moved to Fairfield in 1949. At the time of the shooting, Herman was the vice-president of the Fairfield-Suisun Chamber of Commerce.

The basic facts of the case are as follows: the couple were bickering over a family matter when they went out to dinner. After they returned home, they seemingly had reconciled but Bette said, "Sometimes you make me so mad I could kill you." Herman answered that that would be easy and went to the bedroom, retrieved a .45-caliber pistol and returned to the kitchen.

He started to hand the gun to his wife, which he later described to Fairfield Police Chief Rex Clift as a "more or less joking kind of dare." She grabbed the gun, the couple struggled and it fired. She was shot through the abdomen and died at 2:10 a.m. the next day.

That is the outline of what happened, but the devil is in the details. Now it's important to remember that the following devilish details were provided by Herman, but they are all that have survived.

October 18, 1952, was a Saturday; Herman had worked from 8:00 a.m. to 1:00 p.m. and then hung out at home and did some yard work. During the afternoon, a couple of friends stopped by and they all split two beers. Later in the afternoon, Herman and Bette had a drink of bourbon and water while they were dressing for a dinner engagement with three other friends. At about 7:30 p.m., the friends came over, and two rounds of drinks were served before they traveled from the Freudenberg house on Kentucky Street to Dick's Restaurant (later Dick's Seafood Grotto) on Pennsylvania Avenue, about a mile away.

Now, when they were getting into their friend's car to leave, Bette asked Herman to close the garage door. Herman said there wasn't anything of value in the garage that could be stolen, but Bette again told him to close it, which he did. When Herman got in the car, one of the friends noticed Herman's displeasure at what he perceived as a demeaning tone from his wife and said, "Bette, I think you got a dirty look." They drove in silence to Dick's, and instead of going directly inside, the Freudenbergs stood outside and argued about the Great Garage Door Controversy.

Bette suggested that he pack his bags and leave, and she started to walk away but was coaxed back to the restaurant. Before she entered, she apparently made some remark to Herman that reignited his anger and sent him walking toward home. Bette and one of the other friends drove after him and tried to convince him to come back. Bette even got out and begged on her knees, but he refused. Bette and Herman walked the rest of the way home.

Bette went inside, but Herman got in his car out front and fumed. When he finally went inside, they resumed the quarrel with threats to leave. The "two or three or maybe four drinks" they shared extinguished instead of accelerated the anger. They kissed and discussed how silly it was to bicker over such trivial matters.

It was about 11:00 p.m. when she said, "Herman, sometimes you make me so mad I could kill you."

The details about the gun are illustrative.

It was a .45-caliber semiautomatic pistol Herman had retained from his service in World War II. Importantly, it was not loaded when he pulled it out of the drawer. He loaded a clip into the gun and put a shell in the chamber. He handed the gun to his wife, according to his testimony, in a way that the muzzle was pointed not at her but at an angle. His testimony was that he started to hand it to her and it went off.

As soon as Bette was shot, Herman called the Solano County Hospital, which was about a mile away (across from what in 2025 is the Winery Square shopping center on West Texas Street). He was immediately told to call the Fairfield Hospital, which was about a block from their house at 1107 Kentucky Street (located right across from the Fairfield Civic Center Library). When they got to the hospital, Bette was still conscious and made several statements to her husband to the effect of "Honey, I don't want to die. My back hurts me. Put your arm around my back."

Bette and Herman Freudenberg. *Fairfield Civic Center Library microfilm.*

When the family physician, Dr. Olson, arrived at the hospital, he asked what happened. Herman replied, "It was an accident, Bill," and though Bette was conscious, she made no comment to his reply.

Longtime Fairfield doctors Zimmerman, Rossi and Gauder found that her liver had been lacerated and the transverse colon severed. They did all they could to save her, but Bette died at about 2:10 a.m. from shock, blood loss and the bullet wound.

Alcohol obviously played a part in the tragedy, and an analysis showed Bette's blood alcohol content at 0.163. Herman's was 0.031, although his was taken five hours after Bette was shot.

That five-hour lag before his blood was tested was not the only indication in newspaper articles that Herman Freudenberg Jr. was given deference that wasn't typically extended to those who were not prominent local businesspeople.

Fairfield Police Chief Rex Clift questioned Herman, as did the Solano County Deputy District Attorney, but Herman was not arrested. Indeed, it was only when a grand jury indicted him *three weeks after his wife's death* that the usual accountability started to kick in.

Herman insisted that the shooting was accidental. The tragedy set off an investigation by the Fairfield police department, district attorney's office, county coroner and California Bureau of Criminal Investigation and Identification.

In the American system of justice, defendants are considered innocent until proven guilty in a court of law. However, the court that Herman dealt with for several days after his wife's death was the court of public opinion. To help tamp down what was described in one local newspaper account as "widespread and often inaccurate publicity," Herman agreed to take a lie detector test to back up his assertions.

The three-hour-long test was administered a little more than a week after Bette's death by a state polygraph expert from Sacramento. The following statement was released by the expert: "The undersigned finds no specific indications to support a suspicion that the subject deliberately shot his wife."

It was submitted to the grand jury for examination along with the results of the coroner's inquest. At the inquest, Freudenberg and eight witnesses testified. When asked why he handed his wife a loaded pistol after she had said "Sometimes you make me so mad I could kill you," Freudenberg answered, "Just to call her bluff."

California state criminologists made a paraffin cast of Freudenberg's hands to determine if he was holding the gun when it discharged. The test was to determine if there were powder burns or particles on his hands.

AP Wirephoto

Pretty Mrs. Elizabeth Freudenberg was fatally wounded when her husband handed her a gun during an argument.

Socialite Fatally Shot in Fairfield

Solano Doctor Is First Witness In Freudenberg Trial

Story Of Fatal Solano Quarrel Is Given Jurors

Freudenberg Describes Fatal Struggle for Gun

Bette Freudenberg and headlines about the murder case. *Fairfield Civic Center Library microfilm.*

Similar tests were made of Bette Freudenberg's hands. The tests turned out to be inconclusive.

The autopsy indicated that the .45-caliber bullet that killed Bette took a downward course through her chest.

The grand jury returned an indictment for manslaughter on November 6, 1952. Freudenberg was unable to be arraigned and enter a not guilty plea until December, however, because the first judge assigned to the case had to recuse himself.

More than likely the judge drove a Buick.

The trial started on January 27, 1953. The first witness called was Dr. Olson, who testified that a blood test showed that Bette was in a state of "borderline intoxication." People must have been getting hammered back then, because according to current science, that ain't nowhere close to any border. The legal limit for blood alcohol content for all fifty states in 2025 is .08. Bette was twice that at .163. At that concentration, balance and movement are impaired and there is a risk of nausea, accidents, blackouts and loss of consciousness—not to mention hangovers.

Bette Freudenberg's twelve-year-old daughter from a previous marriage, Phyllis, testified that on the night her mother was shot she heard them arguing and quoted her stepfather as saying, "Why do you make a fool of me in public?" She had already kissed her parents good night, gone to bed and knew nothing more until morning, when she was told her mother was dead.

After Herman Freudenberg and Police Chief Rex Clift testified, it was up to the jury. The six men and six women weighed all of the evidence presented to them and after fifty-seven minutes of deliberation announced they had reached a verdict. Guilty of manslaughter.

When the verdict was read, Herman Freudenberg's mother cried out "Oh, no!" and rushed from the courtroom, where she could be heard sobbing loudly in the hallway. The judge ordered the convicted Fairfielder to come back on February 3 to receive the probation report and pronounce judgment. Freudenberg was remanded into the custody of the sheriff at first, but his counsel asked that he continue on his present bond, which was granted.

On February 3, Freudenberg's defense attorney made an impassioned plea for almost an hour that left many court spectators in tears. Freudenberg wept with his face buried in his hands. Still, the judge denied probation and ruled that Freudenberg be sentenced to serve one to ten years in prison. Freudenberg was remanded into custody to the county jail before being shipped to San Quentin State Prison.

Before he was sent to prison, Bette Freudenberg's former husband and the father of her two now motherless children filed a $150,000 (almost $1.8 million in 2025) damage suit against Herman for "illegally depriving the children of their mother." They had lived with the Freudenbergs until the shooting, after which they lived with their father.

On November 27, 1953, the Third District Appellate Court upheld the Solano County Superior Court manslaughter conviction. All the points lawyers made were shot down, and what it boiled down to was that in view of his own statements as well as his testimony, Herman displayed a lack of due caution and circumspection by bringing a gun to his inebriated wife in a loaded condition with the safety removed and handing it to her barrel first ready to fire.

It is not clear from available records about exactly how much time Freudenberg served. In the 1961 Polk City Directory, he is listed as being back at his old house at 1107 Kentucky—but with a new wife, Joan. He had lots of money left, and he and his new wife bought a home on the Mendocino coast and his daughter attended school in Switzerland and France. In 1964, he sold twelve acres on Oliver Road near Mankas Corner to the Fairfield-Suisun Unified School District. The price tag was $91,112 (over $915,000 in 2025). The district planned to build a third high school there (which did not happen).

Herman L. Freudenberg died in 1989 and is buried at the Sunrise Memorial Cemetery in Vallejo.

1952: Ralph Fong's Murder-for-Hire Scheme

Honestly, what says "I love you" more than bailing your husband out of jail after he was arrested for a plan to murder you for insurance money?

This will take some explaining.

On January 22, 1952, twenty-three-year-old Suisun Valley rancher Ralph Fong picked up two airmen, James Gleason and Angel Velande, as they were hitchhiking back to their quarters on Travis Air Force Base. They were wearing civilian clothes, so Fong evidently did not know they were in the Air Force. Fong asked them if they would like to make some money. When they replied affirmatively, Fong offered them $1,500 and said, "I want you to bump off my wife."

The young airmen played along like they were interested, but after leaving Fong, they immediately notified the base police, who in turn notified Solano County Sheriff Thomas Joyce.

A couple of days later, the airmen met with Fong on Abernathy Lane, and they had a hidden audience of sheriff's deputies. Fong handed them a .30-30 rifle and ammunition and then explained that the plan was to get his wife silhouetted against a lighted window so she could be easily seen and shot.

At this point, the sheriff's department moved in and arrested Fong.

When questioned at the sheriff's office, Fong freely admitted to the plot. He explained that he was having serious financial difficulties. He had come to Solano from San Francisco three years earlier and made a $40,000 down payment on a ranch. Fong's first and only peach and apricot crop was not successful, and he was unable to meet the payments on the mortgage.

That's when he thought of murdering his wife for her $10,000 life insurance policy.

"I love her so much I couldn't shoot her myself," Fong told authorities.

Perhaps owing to the male-dominated newspaper profession, Mabel Fong was described in numerous articles as "attractive," "slender" "petite," "pretty" and "a pertly dressed young beauty." She had a decidedly unusual reaction to the news that her husband had been arrested for masterminding a murder-for-hire plot against her: "I love my husband. We have never quarreled. I don't want the sheriff's office to do anything about this."

Despite her protestations, the sheriff and the district attorney signed a complaint charging Fong with soliciting a person to commit a felony involving murder.

At his June 26 arraignment before Justice of the Peace Georgia Crowley, Fong was released pending trial. Ralph and Mabel held hands throughout the arraignment, and she paid his $1,500 bail. They left the courtroom arm-in-arm, and a photo was snapped of Ralph holding the door for his wife as they exited the courtroom—the model of gentlemanliness.

Some newspaper accounts at the time used paternalistic stereotypes if not downright racist language when describing the happenings in the case:

> *Showing the calm stoicism of her race, pretty Mabel Fong, 21, kept up the centuries old tradition of intense loyalty that runs in Chinese families when she appeared in court to hear charges that her husband had conspired to have her murdered because he needed money.*

Suisun Valley rancher Ralph Fong with his wife, Mabel, whom he tried to have killed in a murder-for-hire plot. *Newspapers.com.*

At a preliminary hearing on February 1, perhaps the whole sordid situation became a little more real to Mabel, as she was reported to have bitten her lips and looked down at her hands during the proceeding. That's because an audio recording between her husband and chief criminal investigator for the sheriff's office Stanley Emerson was played in open court. Emerson asked Fong to tell "the complete story."

Fong's voice was alternately calm and jerky as Emerson set the stage by having Fong talk about his financial woes, picking up the airmen and discussing the $10,000 life insurance policy. Then he asked, "How did you plan to eliminate her?"

"I couldn't bring myself to do it, so I was going to hire somebody to do it. I picked up two men. I didn't know they were airmen at the time. I had it planned for January 24th, but something came up and I took my wife to a show that night. Then I contacted the men again and they were to kill her on the night of January 25th."

Mabel Fong mainly kept her eyes averted except for moments when she looked up at the recorder and frowned.

James Gleason and Angel Velande testified about meeting Fong and receiving the rifle from him. They also said Fong had taken them to his ranch house to meet his wife so they would know who to shoot.

Although Justice of the Peace Georgia Crowley ordered Fong held for Superior Court action, he was allowed to remain at liberty under the earlier bond.

On March 3, Fong pleaded innocent and innocent by reason of insanity before Judge Harlow Greenwood. A little more than two weeks later, he changed his mind and pleaded guilty to solicitation of murder and was referred to the probation department. Judge Greenwood sentenced Fong to serve four months in jail, pay a fine of $1,500 at the rate of $75 per month after he was released from jail and be placed on probation for five years.

While he was sentenced in April, Fong didn't begin serving his prescribed jail time until November. The judge agreed to let him harvest his prune crop first.

In the 1960s, Ralph Fong was hired by Ed Lippstreu of Solano County Title, and then from 1965 to 1968 he ran his own realty firm. Then in 1968, Fong and two partners were held by Mexican authorities in connection with the cashing of stolen U.S. stock certificates. He was also sued by Vaca Valley Bank for defaulting on a $18,000 promissory note.

Apparently, Fong learned a lesson, because there is nothing in the historical record suggesting Fong tried to have his wife bumped off to pay for lawyer's fees or the defaulted loan.

3

OFFICER DOWN!

A common police radio code is 10-00 (Ten Double Zero) which means "officer down, all patrols respond." Officers are trained to respond to such calls by rapidly transporting wounded colleagues, preserving evidence and being acutely aware of safety protocols in a high-stress environment. In that scenario, the muscle memory of training kicks in and the officers act accordingly.

One of the hardest parts of being a law enforcement officer is dealing with the loss of a comrade taken while in the line of duty. The Solano County Peace Officers Memorial Garden, located in Fairfield on Union Avenue near the Solano County Sheriff's Office and the county jail, was dedicated in 1990. It is the location for an annual memorial service for all officers killed in the line of duty in Solano County since 1892.

The following are stories of some of the officers killed and one who was wounded.

Solano County Sheriff's Investigator Hale Humphrey

On March 15, 1963, a crime spree by two teenagers, eighteen-year-old Richard Price and sixteen-year-old Jack Lemar Sikes, resulted in the death of two law enforcement officers. They were California Highway Patrolman Charles Sorenson and Solano County Sheriff's Investigator Hale Humphrey.

KILLED — Deputy Sheriff Hale Humphrey of Solano County.

SHOT TO DEATH — Highway Patrolman Charles Sorenson, 32.

Top: The Solano County Law Enforcement Memorial on Union Avenue. *Tony Wade.*

Bottom: *Left*, Deputy Sheriff Hale Humphrey; *right*, California Highway Patrol Officer Charles Sorenson. *Fairfield Civic Center Library microfilm.*

At about 4:30 p.m. on that fateful day, Price and Sikes went into a gas station in Lodi. William Kempe, who was visiting relatives in Lodi, came out of the bathroom as he was waiting to get his car serviced. One of the youths told him to get back into the bathroom and pointed a snub-nosed .25-caliber automatic pistol at him. Kempe thought it was a joke and pushed the youth, who responded by shooting Kempe in his thigh.

The pair then sped off in a car stolen from the co-owner of the gas station. The gas station owner gave chase in Kempe's car and followed the thieves down State Route 12 toward Rio Vista. Patrolman Sorenson received a radio alert about the car and began his own pursuit. At the Rio Vista Bridge, the teens lost control of the stolen car and hit a telephone pole.

Price and Sikes ran to an abandoned house, and Sorenson followed with his gun drawn. When the officer stepped around a corner of the house, Price shot and killed him with a bullet to the neck. He and Sikes then took off in the dead officer's car and hit speeds of up to 130 miles an hour.

Sheriff's officers had set up a roadblock six miles east of Fairfield using two trucks and a car. Price and Sikes slammed into the roadblock and a hail of bullets. Hale Humphrey, who had been firing a shotgun from behind his car, was crushed to death.

In 2019, Stanley Emerson, who was then one hundred years old, remembered the incident very clearly. Hale Humphrey had been his partner. "One day Hale came running and said, 'We have a stolen CHP car from Rio Vista with a cop killer coming!' I went to get my pistol and saw him driving away. I got another car, and I arrived just after the impact. When Hale was killed, he was between two patrol cars with a sawed-off shotgun. He was a good man."

Price and Sikes, who were both wearing seatbelts, were pulled from the wreckage and taken to the County Hospital. They were held there under guard for days, and Price shattered his leg cast trying to get out of bed. Sikes was released from the hospital sooner and was confined in Juvenile Hall.

Price had served more than a year in a reformatory for car theft and was sought in connection with two armed holdups at the time of his Solano County crimes. Sikes was a runaway whose father and stepmother called him a dangerous incorrigible. Since he was a juvenile, Sikes was sent to the California Youth Authority.

At his funeral, held in the Armijo High School auditorium, Hale was eulogized as an "outstanding man in his prime."

The case against Richard Price went to trial in August 1963, and the evidence of the crime spree was laid out methodically. It was capped off with the showing of a television interview from station KPIX that was filmed when Price was in the hospital in March. In the video, Price's face was bruised and scratched, and he admitted his guilt freely. He said he would not seek the services of an attorney to represent him.

He also said that anyone who drives into something at 110 miles an hour does not want to live.

Price was found guilty, sentenced to death and sent to Death Row at San Quentin. In 1965, however, his conviction was overturned based on the Escobedo ruling. That 1964 Illinois case involved a defendant denied the right to counsel. In a 5–4 decision, the Supreme Court said that police must advise a suspect of his right to remain silent and obtain a lawyer before taking a statement that might later be used to convict him.

Price was retried in August 1966, and his attorney argued that while his client did kill Sorenson, he didn't have the necessary premeditation to qualify for the gas chamber. He also floated the defense of diminished capacity. He argued that because of his emotional immaturity and impaired reasoning, Price was incapable of premeditating and deliberating on how to kill the officer chasing him.

The judge did not buy either argument. Price was convicted of first-degree murder for the death of Sorenson and second-degree murder for

The sign honoring Hale Humphrey on Highway 12. *Tony Wade.*

the death of Humphrey and sent to the penitentiary. He was paroled from Soledad Prison in September 1978.

Hale Humphrey, only forty-two years old when he was killed, had served in the army and then as a Fairfield police officer before making the lateral move to the sheriff's office. He met his wife, Betty, when he pulled her over. The next day, he showed up at her office and asked her out. As an investigator, Humphrey covered everything from narcotics busts to child welfare calls to sheep rustling.

He was a sharpshooter and either won or placed in the top five in statewide annual law enforcement shooting competitions. At the Solano County shooting match between different law enforcement agencies, the Hale Humphrey Memorial Trophy was presented for the first time in 1964.

In honor of their sacrifice, portions of Highway 12 were named after Sorenson and Humphrey. They are the Officer Charles "Chuck" Sorenson Memorial Highway between State Route 16 and Brannan Island Road and the Solano County Deputy Sheriff Hale Humphrey Memorial Highway between Fairfield and Suisun City.

FAIRFIELD POLICE SERGEANT ART KOCH

Art Koch (pronounced "coach"), the first Fairfield police officer killed in the line of duty, was born on February 3, 1950, in St. Louis, Missouri. He joined the U.S. Marine Corps, served in Vietnam and was honorably discharged in 1972 after reaching the rank of sergeant as a radar technician. Koch was a California Highway Patrolman for eight years before coming to Fairfield as a police officer in 1979.

Instead of leading off with the tragic details of the murder, it seems more fitting to talk about what kind of person Art Koch was. Too often victims of violent crime are defined solely by the act that cut their lives short.

The following statements were provided by Art's widow, Barbara Koch:

> *On the night that Art passed away, we had been busily packing our trailer to leave the next day to go camping after Art's shift. That was our favorite activity to do as a family. We loved our little trailer, and we shared some of our best times camping with the kids.*
>
> *I was told by strangers that even though Art had stopped them for a violation, he always treated them kindly and fairly, with a smile on his face.*

Fairfield Police Sergeant Art Koch. *Public domain.*

> *He truly loved his job and everything that it demanded, but he never brought the hard times home with him. He was the true definition of a family man. He adored his children, who were eleven, seven and two when he was taken from us. They have all grown up to be amazing adults, but there will always be a huge void of what could have been for them. My seven grandkids talk often about Grandpa Art and still sense the pain when their parents talk about him.*
>
> *He was playful, had a great sense of humor and very rarely became irritated. He loved sports and played tennis, basketball and golf. One of his favorite events was the Pig Bowl, an annual football game with opposing police departments playing each other. It was renamed The Art Koch Pig Bowl in his honor after his death.*
>
> *Although Art's death has affected my family so incredibly, I also know that it had a profound effect on his fellow officers. He was just such a genuinely kind person and is missed every day.*

Fairfield Police Chief Charles Huchel provided a glimpse of what Art was like to those who did not know him in Koch's eulogy:

> *He was the kind of man who liked to be where the action was, in the thick of things. He gave his life protecting citizens so that they may go on being husbands, fathers, daughters, sons and friends. He was the kind of man that would try to breakdance with his son, would take his daughter swimming and throw her in the air. He was the kind of man who wrote his mother a warning ticket on her birthday. In the remarks section he wrote: "In violation of being the best mother in the world. Happy birthday."*

So here are the tragic details.

On July 28, 1984, Berkeley Way residents called police because a volatile neighbor, a legless Vietnam veteran named Stanley Verketis, was firing a rifle randomly in their neighborhood. A rookie officer arrived at the scene and waited for Koch to arrive as backup. Koch was just leaving his car when Verketis shot him in the chest with an 8mm Mauser rifle. Although Koch was wearing a standard-issue bulletproof vest, it was not designed to

The 1981 Fairfield Department of Public Safety Pig Bowl team. Art Koch is in the second row, far right. The annual event was renamed for him after his tragic murder. *History of the Solano County Sheriff's Office Facebook page.*

stop shots from high-power rifles, and the bullet tore through his chest and exited out the small of his back. Koch fell forward over a bicycle and then pulled himself behind his vehicle for protection.

He lay down by his car, but it was twenty minutes before paramedics and firefighters were able to rescue him, as Verketis was firing indiscriminately. The first responders then improvised a solution to extricate Koch. Firefighters drove a truck next to the house and shot a stream of water at it while a paramedic scrambled out of a medical truck and dragged Koch into the vehicle. From there they sped to Intercommunity Hospital.

Verketis stayed in the house for several hours and kept randomly shooting. Some of his neighbors were evacuated by Fairfield's Special Activities and Felony Enforcement (SAFE) team, but many were trapped in their homes. Negotiators were finally able to talk Verketis into surrendering after promising him that he would receive hospital care. He surrendered and was arrested at around 2:20 a.m. the next day. A little over an hour later, Officer Arthur Koch died of massive internal injuries caused by the gunshot wound to the chest.

In their search of the house, officers found other weapons, including seven other rifles, a shotgun, a crossbow and a blowgun.

The shock of Koch's senseless murder was exacerbated by the fact that it was his last night on patrol. He was going to go camping with his family and upon his return would then start work as a sergeant.

Stanley Verketis was well known to law enforcement in Fairfield and surrounding areas. A *Daily Republic* article from June 27, 1966, was titled "Several People Jailed During Weekend." One of those listed was eighteen-year-old Stanley Karl Verketis, who was picked up on charges of furnishing liquor to minors following a house party.

In 1970, the *Napa Valley Register* reported Stanley Verketis and his brother Patrick were arrested by the Napa County Sheriff's Department near Lake Berryessa's Markley Cove resort. Authorities found two loaded pistols under the front car seat, and the siblings were hit with concealed weapons charges.

On May 5, 1971, officers responded to a fight report and had to mace Stanley and a different brother, Stephen, to subdue and handcuff them. The brothers were arrested for assault on a police officer, resisting arrest, disturbing the peace and profanity in the presence of a woman.

When he was in Vietnam in 1968, Private First Class Stanley Verketis, a paratrooper with the 173rd Airborne Brigade's 2nd Battalion, repeatedly found booby traps that would have spelled disaster for his comrades in arms. He found one that was big enough to kill ten men. One he didn't find in October of that year exploded and threw him thirty-five feet, which cost him both of his legs.

Verketis reportedly didn't like using his prosthetic legs or wheelchair and only did so when he went out to the store. Instead, he would drag himself around using his arms.

Theories about why Verketis started shooting that day included distress over his father's recent death, feeling despondent because his wife left him and took their children to Sacramento or that he was having a Vietnam flashback at the time.

Whatever the reason, he was responsible for an officer's death and would be called to account for his actions.

Ramona Garrett, a 1970 Armijo High grad, had come to the district attorney's office in Fairfield that July and was described as an excellent trial lawyer. She was assigned to the prosecution of Stanley Verketis.

Judge Ramona Garrett, who, as a young attorney, prosecuted Stanley Verketis. *Fairfield Civic Center Library microfilm.*

Plaque at the Art Koch Range and Training facility. *Public domain.*

"About the third week I was there, I had a burglary case and met the investigating officer I'd be working with. His name was Officer Arthur Koch," Garrett said. "We did the trial, I lost, we shook hands and he went on his way. I heard within a day or two he got shot. I was going to go visit him at Intercommunity Hospital, but the next day the paper said that he'd died."

Verketis's attorney was successful in getting the trial venue changed to Contra Costa County because of extensive local news coverage in Fairfield. During the 1986 trial, Verketis's attorney tried to show that his client didn't intend to kill the officer but was having a Vietnam flashback.

Ramona Garrett argued that Verketis did intend to kill Koch because he was depressed over life events and hoped to die using the "suicide by cop" method. In December 1986, the jury deadlocked, and a mistrial was declared by the judge.

Defense arguments and testimony about Verketis's posttraumatic stress disorder from his time in Vietnam backfired in the retrial, as he was seen by some jurors as being too dangerous to be in society. After seven hours of deliberations, they found him guilty of first-degree murder with special circumstances. On March 3, 1988, he was sentenced to life in prison without the possibility of parole.

Stanley Verketis died in prison on March 28, 2017, at the age of sixty-nine.

In 2008, the City of Fairfield dedicated the Fairfield Police Art Koch Training Facility, a thirty-nine-thousand-square-foot state-of-the-art training facility with indoor rifle and pistol ranges.

In 2024, on the fortieth anniversary of Koch's end of watch, the Fairfield Police Department issued the following statement about their fallen comrade.

> *July 28, 1984, is a day the department and the City of Fairfield will never forget. Sergeant Art Koch was a loving husband, father, and a dedicated*

police officer. He cared greatly for this community and the fact that he died protecting it was a clear demonstration of his love.

We remember Sergeant Koch every day, but as we honor him on this 40th anniversary of his tragic passing in the line of duty, we're also appreciative of his sacrifice. Although he may no longer be here, physically, he lives on through his beautiful family and in each of us—in how we interact with, embrace, collaborate, and look out for each other. We think he would be proud to see a community united.

SOLANO COUNTY DEPUTY SHERIFF JOSE CISNEROS

Law enforcement officers never know which call could be their last. A seemingly routine call can turn tragic. That's what happened to Deputy Sheriff Jose Cisneros.

On August 25, 1985, Solano County Sheriff's dispatch received a call from a resident on Cherry Glen Road in Vacaville saying someone in a gray 1985 Chevrolet van parked outside their house was throwing stuff from their vehicle. It turned out to be cassette tapes and the vehicle's ownership paperwork.

Deputy Sheriff Jose Cisneros, a fourteen-year veteran, responded to the call and looked for the van. At about 5:25 p.m., he found it near the intersection of Cherry Glen and Pleasant Valley Roads in Vacaville. Inside the van were eighteen-year-old John Davis Kirk and his seventeen-year-old accomplice Michael Remington. Kirk had backed the van approximately sixty yards off the road into an adjacent field. Cisneros drove his patrol car into the field, stopping it about ten yards away from the van with the two vehicles facing each other. Unbeknownst to Cisneros, the pair were wanted for a series of crimes in San Pablo.

Cisneros got out of his car and walked toward the van. Remington got out of the van, pointed a shotgun at Cisneros and demanded that he remove his gun belt. Cisneros unbuckled his belt, and Remington fired one shot into the ground and, fifteen to thirty seconds later, shot Cisneros in the face from a range of about eight feet. Cisneros's eyeglasses flew off his face and landed thirty-one feet away. The blast killed him instantly.

The perpetrators then sped off in the van. California Highway Patrol officers responded and gave chase, and Remington began shooting at them. The high-speed chase moved through Winters and east toward Davis. The van finally pulled into an almond orchard just outside Winters, and the two suspects surrendered.

Second guessing began almost immediately following the shooting of Cisneros. Why was he alone? The sheriff's office responded that it was standard operating procedure for officers to patrol alone.

A rather damning detail was revealed shortly afterward. Cisneros was not aware of a law enforcement bulletin issued to nine nearby law enforcement agencies that would have warned him he was investigating armed suspects and not just joyriding litterers.

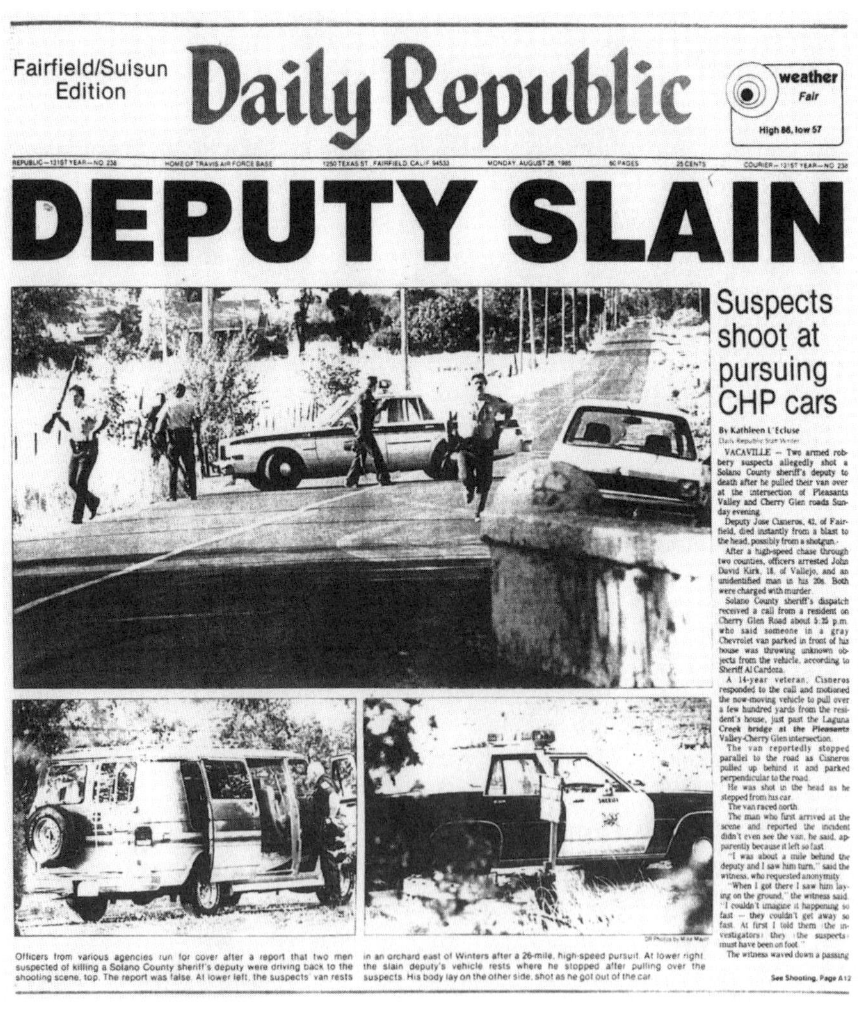

Fairfield/Suisun Edition

Daily Republic

weather
Fair
High 86, low 57

REPUBLIC—131ST YEAR—NO. 238 | HOME OF TRAVIS AIR FORCE BASE | 1250 TEXAS ST., FAIRFIELD, CALIF. 94533 | MONDAY, AUGUST 26, 1985 | 60 PAGES | 25 CENTS | COURIER—131ST YEAR—NO. 238

DEPUTY SLAIN

Officers from various agencies run for cover after a report that two men suspected of killing a Solano County sheriff's deputy were driving back to the shooting scene, top. The report was false. At lower left, the suspects' van rests in an orchard east of Winters after a 26-mile, high-speed pursuit. At lower right the slain deputy's vehicle rests where he stopped after pulling over the suspects. His body lay on the other side, shot as he got out of the car.

Suspects shoot at pursuing CHP cars

By Kathleen L'Ecluse
Daily Republic Staff Writer

VACAVILLE — Two armed robbery suspects allegedly shot a Solano County sheriff's deputy to death after he pulled their van over at the intersection of Pleasants Valley and Cherry Glen roads Sunday evening.

Deputy Jose Cisneros, 42, of Fairfield, died instantly from a blast to the head, possibly from a shotgun.

After a high-speed chase through two counties, officers arrested John David Kirk, 18, of Vallejo, and an unidentified man in his 20s. Both were charged with murder.

Solano County sheriff's dispatch received a call from a resident on Cherry Glen Road about 5:25 p.m. who said someone in a gray Chevrolet van parked in front of his house was throwing unknown objects from the vehicle, according to Sheriff Al Cardoza.

A 14-year veteran, Cisneros responded to the call and motioned the now-moving vehicle to pull over a few hundred yards from the resident's house, just past the Laguna Creek bridge at the Pleasants Valley-Cherry Glen intersection.

The van reportedly stopped parallel to the road as Cisneros pulled up behind it and parked perpendicular to the road.

He was shot in the head as he stepped from his car.

The van raced north.

The man who first arrived at the scene and reported the incident didn't even see the van, he said, apparently because it left so fast.

"I was about a mile behind the deputy and I saw him turn," said the witness, who requested anonymity.

"When I got there I saw him laying on the ground," the witness said. "I couldn't imagine it happening so fast — they couldn't get away so fast. At first I told them (the investigators) they (the suspects) must have been on foot."

The witness waved down a passing

See Shooting, Page A12

The *Daily Republic* front page the day after Deputy Sheriff Jose Cisneros was killed. *Fairfield Civic Center Library microfilm.*

Deputy Sheriff Jose Cisneros. *History of the Solano County Sheriff's Office Facebook page.*

The bulletin, issued by San Pablo Police, warned officers from nine different cities to be on the lookout for a van allegedly stolen at gunpoint earlier in the day from a man at a San Pablo shopping area. Nine was the maximum number of bulletins that could be sent out at one time. Vallejo could have relayed the bulletin to other Solano agencies, but they were not directed to do so.

While it was unlikely that Cisneros would have received any useful information in the few seconds from the time he radioed the van's license number for a DMV check to the time he was shot, going forward, bulletins on major crimes from Contra Costa were transmitted to all Solano County agencies.

Kirk and Remington had met in 1984, and they decided they wanted to leave the area but needed money. They stole weapons, including antique firearms, swords and a saber from Kirk's parents' home in Vallejo. They also stole the van.

They were both charged with murdering Cisneros as well as grand theft of the weapons in Vallejo, robbery of the van in San Pablo, vehicle theft and assault with a deadly weapon for shooting at the CHP officers during the chase.

Jurors convicted Remington of second-degree murder and eight lesser counts in December 1987. Calling the slaying "calculated and cowardly," Superior Court Judge John A. DeRonde sent Remington to prison in April 1988 for thirty-one years to life—the maximum sentence allowed.

In January 1988, Kirk pleaded guilty to armed voluntary manslaughter and seven lesser charges. He also was given the maximum sentence of seventeen years in prison.

Elsa Cisneros Shares Memories of Her Late Husband

Joe Cisneros was a complex and interesting man. He had a zest for life that I see reflected in our daughter, Cassandra. He was curious about everything, and when he had an interest he delved into it to the utmost extent. One of his early hobbies was tropical fish. Over time, one ten-gallon tank grew into a spare bedroom full of tanks of various sizes, and a six-foot-long tank in the family room. His special interest was in South American cichlids. We bought many books and became quite knowledgeable about them.

Typical of Joe, he became great friends with the owners of a small pet store and joined a tropical fish club, where we made more friends.

Joe was very sociable and loved laughter and good conversation. He considered himself an atheist and enjoyed discussions with a few of the more religious deputies about the validity of the Bible and its stories. The conversations were always civil, never devolving into disrespect, but his logic always seemed to win the day—at least in his mind!

He took a big interest in the subject of UFOs, and I still have some of his books on the subject. This was during the time he discovered Isaac Asimov's books, which piqued Joe's interest in the subject. He even invested in some good binoculars so that he could scan the skies when he worked night shift. He often spoke about how beautiful the night sky was when viewed out in the country. He even told me he would love to have a UFO encounter. I remember saying to him, "but they might kidnap you." His response was that was okay, he would find it fascinating!

Another interest he had was in cycling. He went from just riding a bit for exercise to full-on cycling hundred-mile runs called centuries. Early on, he bent a bicycle frame going up a steep hill. He realized he needed a bike more suited to his big frame, and a man from Dixon crafted one more suitable for him.

In December 1974, Joe had an accident in which a defective holster caused his firearm to fire as he was unholstering it. It broke his femur, and he spent months in a body cast. The following summer he was still recovering at home, walking with the help of a cane. Our little neighborhood cul-de-sac decided to have a block party for the Fourth of July. All went well and everybody had fun socializing and eating until it began to get dark.

We stepped outside to chat with neighbors and check on the kids when we realized the court had filled up with people not from our neighborhood, mostly teenagers. It was beginning to get unruly with too many kids jammed together with the probability of liquor involved. Joe decided that it was time to break the party up. I told him not to confront them as he was still recovering and to just call the police, but he was determined to handle it. I still have this memory of him limping, leaning on his cane, disappearing into the crowd.

I don't know what he said or how much the kids resisted, but my worries were unfounded—the kids started to disperse and the party broke up with no incidents. I guess if you have a good command presence you can get things done!

Joe loved to fish and always wanted a fishing boat and saved for years to buy one. He used to go stream fishing and camping with Cassandra often. His favorite place to fish was in Suisun Bay, where the mothball fleet was anchored. He said there were lots of shadowy dark places for fish to hang out, and he had good luck there.

After Joe was killed, we had his ashes scattered over that area. Tony Hunley, who was a Fairfield police officer, flew us over that spot. I am a Nervous Nellie about flying in small planes as it is, and I didn't realize he would have to stall the engine in order to open the door to release the ashes. What a scary moment that was—suspended over deep water with no engine sounds! Thankfully another Fairfield police officer and friend, Tony Ford, was with us, and he did the honors. Had I known that fact about stalling the plane in advance, Joe would probably still be sitting on the mantel, forty years later.

Fairfield Police Detective Mark Smith— Grateful to Be Alive

At 1:42 a.m. on February 24, 1989, the Oakland Police Department, with assistance from Fairfield police, went to search the home of Roberto Adolpho Ramirez on Hayes Street in Fairfield. One of the Fairfield officers was Detective Mark Smith.

"In the late 1980s, Bay Area law enforcement cracked down on crime using task forces. The big-time drug dealers moved to the suburbs but sold drugs in the larger cities," Smith said. "Ramirez was a model citizen in Fairfield but was moving kilos of cocaine in the Bay Area."

Police identified themselves in English and Spanish and then attempted to force their way into the house. Ramirez fired a .357-caliber revolver at the police, hitting Smith and Oakland Officer Marc Burrell.

"The house had a room built into the garage, which was at a ninety-degree angle to the front door and Ramirez's son was sleeping in there. He actually stood over his son's bed when he shot out the windows sideways at the officers that were at the front door," Smith said. "I was at the opposite corner looking toward the back of the house to see if anybody came out of the windows."

Mark Smith

Fairfield detective was in critical but stable condition Friday night

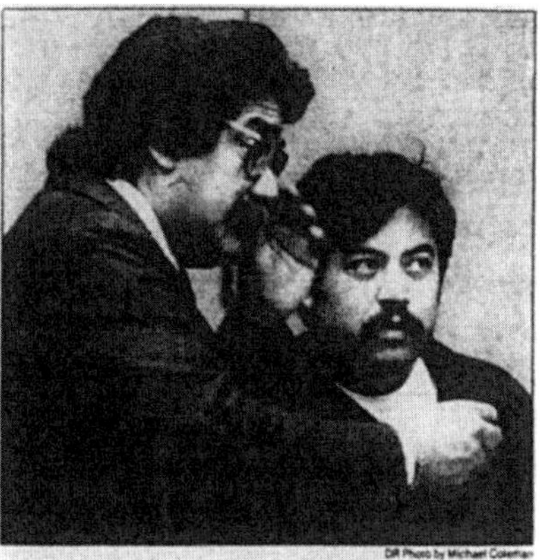
Roberto Aldopho Ramirez, accused of shooting two police officers, appears with court interpreter Jim Flores as charges are read against him in Northern Solano Municipal Court Monday.

Top: Fairfield Police Detective Mark Smith. *Fairfield Civic Center Library microfilm.*

Bottom: Roberto Ramirez (*right*) and his interpreter in court. *Fairfield Civic Center Library microfilm.*

Smith was knocked to the ground by the force of the shot, which went between the panels of his bulletproof vest. His aorta, liver, pancreas and large bowel sustained serious damage.

"Most doctors that look at the record told me it was a 99 percent fatal injury. With an abdominal injury, if it doesn't kill you, the infections usually do."

Officer Burrell was shot in the arm and treated and released from NorthBay Medical Center. Smith spent the next three months there.

After shooting Smith and Burrell, Ramirez holed up in his house. At 3:45 a.m., he surrendered and used the same son whose bed he had shot over as a human shield. A search of the house yielded forty ounces of cocaine worth $30,000 (over $76,000 in 2025).

Ramirez was charged with two counts of attempted murder, assault with a deadly weapon and possession of narcotics with intent to sell. His wife, Eladia, was also arrested when she later tried to empty their bank account of $19,000. She was charged with possession of cocaine. Before the Ramirezes could be tried, they skipped bail and have never been brought to justice.

Smith discovered the county had not gone after the property after Ramirez skipped town. Due to a leaking underground gasoline tank that contaminated the soil, it was not worth the bond. "Ramirez was allowed to post a $500,000 property bond straight to the county on a gas station in East Los Angeles that his friend owned that was appraised at $750,000. He didn't have to go through a bail bondsman, who would have done his due diligence to determine if the property was actually worth that much. His judge later apologized to me."

In search of Justice, Smith contacted TV shows *America's Most Wanted* and *Unsolved Mysteries*, and the latter did a profile that aired on December 8, 1995. In 2006, Ramirez's daughter, interviewed by Fairfield and Stanislaus County investigators, said her father died in Mexico, but that has not been proven.

Smith has a few lingering effects from the shooting but looks back on his extended hospital stay as the grueling part: "Getting shot once is nowhere near as painful as the treatment. I was constantly being poked and prodded. I had an IV that they had to redo every three days, and they used up all the veins in my arms so they had to start sticking needles in my feet. I never had a fear of getting shot again, but after spending three months there, I do have a fear of hospitals."

In 1991, Smith retired from police work but three years later began working for the Stanislaus County District Attorney's Office, where he stayed for nearly eighteen years before retiring.

4

THE MISSING, THE FOUND, THE UNSOLVED

He who commits injustice is ever made more wretched than he who suffers it.
—Plato

The concept of closure in psychological terms describes an individual's desire for a clear, firm answer or peaceful resolution to a question or problem to avert ambiguity. When it comes to applying that principle in tragic real-life situations like kidnappings and murder, the word seems small, insufficient, and is seen by some as a myth.

In 1993, social psychologists Arie Kruglanski, Donna Webster and Adena Klem developed the Need For Closure Scale (NFCS), a questionnaire that measures the intensity or lack of it for people who value order and dislike ambiguity.

Whether myth or science, when a crime is committed, the actions of loved ones, law enforcement and the general public are all geared toward finding out the truth. Sometimes that happens and sometimes it does not. The level of peace that closure brings to the involved parties is subjective.

Clark Toshiro Handa
Kidnapped from His Bedroom

The *Daily Republic* headline "Boy Kidnapped from his Room" sent intense shockwaves of fear throughout Fairfield and neighboring communities and

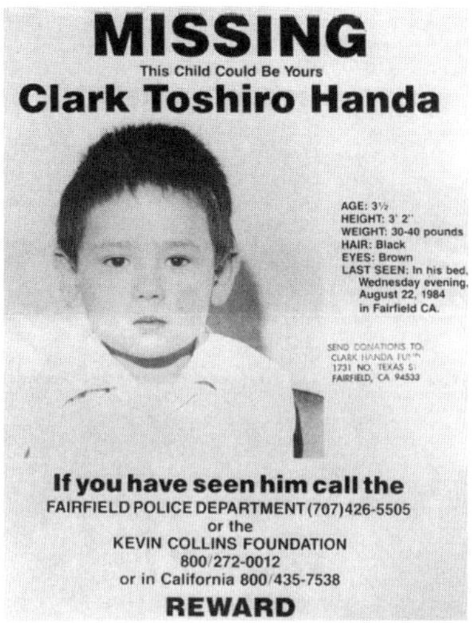

then quickly spread across the country. On the morning of August 23, 1984, three-and-a-half-year-old Clark Toshiro Handa was discovered to be missing from his family's house on Magellan Road (which is now Auto Mall Parkway), and the window in his bedroom was open. The police were called, and Clark's separated parents, Ron and Linda, and his grandfather Harry Smith Jr. helped in the search.

Linda Handa discovered an envelope in the child's bed, and inside was a ransom note. No dollar amount was given by police, but it was "quite a bit" an FBI agent was quoted as saying. A kidnapping for ransom usually targets people of means, but the Handas described themselves as poor people and didn't know anyone who had anything against them.

The ransom note gave a rendezvous point for the delivery of the money and the safe return of the child. The Fairfield police, FBI and Solano County Sheriff's Office made plans to deliver the money, but no one appeared at the designated spot. Authorities waited until midnight before calling off the money drop.

Top: A poster for missing Fairfield child Clark Toshiro Handa. *Christine Donahue Brimer.*

Bottom: A 1984 Child ID that many parents got for their children after Clark Toshiro Handa's kidnapping. *Christine Donahue Brimer.*

Michael Fejarang, the killer of Clark Toshiro Handa. *Public domain.*

Clark Handa's face was printed on flyers and milk cartons, searches were conducted and leads followed. Terrified parents in the area had their children photographed and fingerprinted. The only leads in the case turned out to be false, and the case grew cold.

Years and then decades passed. From time to time, age-enhanced photos of Clark Handa were released, but still there was no luck in finding him or his kidnapper.

In 2011, the Fairfield Police Department's Cold Case Unit, with the assistance of the FBI, took a fresh look at the case. They hit paydirt, as they were able to identify a suspect. In 2016, Michael Anthony Blas Fejarang was charged with the murder of Clark along with special circumstances because the murder occurred during the commission of a kidnapping. Fejarang was also charged with kidnapping for ransom.

When he was charged with Clark's murder, Fejarang was already serving a twenty-six-year prison sentence for a 2002 Solano County child molestation case and was incarcerated at Valley State Prison in Chowchilla. Back in 1984, Fejarang was a twenty-three-year-old Fairfield resident and a friend of the Handa family.

Detectives determined that Fejarang planned the abduction of Clark Handa, killed him just days after the kidnapping and buried the body on the outskirts of Vacaville. Fejarang couldn't remember the location of the unmarked grave. He also said he had accomplices, a woman and a man, but the woman was dead, and he didn't know where the man was.

Fejarang pleaded no contest to first-degree murder in August 2017 and was sentenced to an additional twenty-five years to life in prison, to be served concurrently with his child molestation sentence.

The Handa family had some measure of closure after thirty-three years but were still unable to bury their beloved boy, as his body has never been found.

AMANDA NIKKI CAMPBELL DISAPPEARS

On December 27, 1991, a four-year-old apple-cheeked girl disappeared from her Fairfield neighborhood. Amanda Nicole Campbell, nicknamed Nikki, went to a nearby friend's house with her older brother. Evidently, she decided to go to another friend's house from there and never came home. Her parents, Jim and Anne Campbell, had only started allowing their children to visit neighborhood friends a short time before Nikki's disappearance. The only thing they found was her pink and purple bicycle near a gate leading to an empty lot around the corner from the Campbell home.

Word spread quickly, and family members joined law enforcement searching the neighborhoods and fields around Fairfield. Tips came in, but though promising at first, they did not pan out. Thousands of flyers were distributed, rewards for information were offered, and the FBI worked with local officials, but the dogged efforts to find Nikki were fruitless.

According to media reports at the time, a scent dog traced Nikki toward the busy city streets that lead to Interstate 80. The dog picked up her trail on Larchmont Drive, went down Oliver Road and through the drive-thru McDonald's about a mile away. It lost her scent on Travis Boulevard near the westbound I-80 onramp.

Eventually, a prime suspect emerged—an Oakland man named Timothy Bindner. There were so many unusual and damning things about Bindner that a book could be written. In fact, one was. It is called *Stalemate: A Shocking True Story of Child Abduction and Murder* by John Philpin.

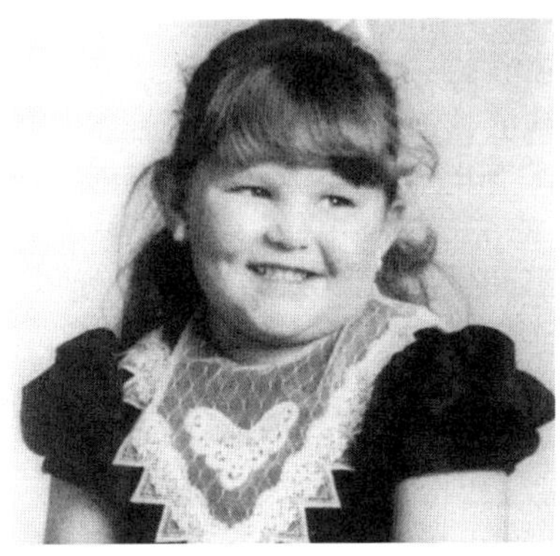

Amanda "Nikki" Campbell, who disappeared from her Fairfield home in 1991. *Public domain.*

Bindner was an odd duck to say the least. For example, he used to work at a crematorium and wrote fan fiction/poetry about his experience: "Diaperless infants with unmoving chests. They burned, side by side, at the front of the oven. Before I washed the white dust off my hands, I tasted of their souls."

He was an enthusiastic volunteer in the investigations of several missing Bay Area little girls, including Amber Swartz-Garcia and Micheala Garecht, who both disappeared in 1988.

In 1989, Contra Costa County authorities charged Bindner with two misdemeanor child molestation counts accusing him of annoying and harassing two young girls by offering rides in his van. Inside the van, police found a book titled *Infanticide*, photos of several young girls and fliers about missing ones. On the back of the Amber Swartz Garcia flier Bindner had written: "I love you, Amber. You were my first and I tried so hard for you."

The cases never went to trial.

Bindner often visited the gravesite of five-year-old Angela Bugay in Pleasant Hill. A bloodhound sniffed the scent of Amanda Campbell there. A week later, authorities saw Bindner climbing from a ravine near Campbell's house, and a bloodhound detected her scent in Bindner's car.

Bindner always claimed that he was simply trying to help and had nothing to do with the disappearances of any of the young girls he searched for. Now, in fairness, there is evidence of him simply wanting to be of help in other ways. In the 1989 Loma Prieta earthquake, Bindner was presented with a framed certificate from the California Highway Patrol for helping people trapped in the collapsed Cypress Street overpass in Oakland. The following year, he helped save a school from burning down during the devastating fires in the Oakland and Berkeley hills.

Bindner was intelligent and knew that he was considered a suspect by several law enforcement agencies, including the FBI. He would often contact specific officers in a taunting sort of manner while protesting his innocence.

In March 1992, Fairfield Police Lieutenant Harold Sagan started playing a chess game by mail with Bindner, who had been writing the department regular letters. But then, on the advice of counsel, Bindner stopped the game before it could finish.

Then authorities assumed they checkmated the suspect.

In December 1992, armed with a search warrant and a bloodhound, sixteen Fairfield police officers examined Bindner's North Oakland home for eight hours and left with four boxes of materials and papers. The press had been tipped off, and the Fairfield police defended the search as a normal and logical step in an investigation.

After the highly publicized search, Bindner and his family were subjected to threats and intimidation and kicked out of several public places. In June 1993, Bindner sued the Fairfield Police Department for $25 million and named Sagan for saying that he was the prime suspect in the Amanda Campbell case.

In 1995, a judge dismissed the case and said that while he was distressed by the Fairfield police making a media circus of the search of Bindner's house, no federal law was broken.

An age-enhanced image of Amanda "Nikki" Campbell. *Fairfield Civic Center Library microfilm.*

The judge also said he was distressed by Bindner's "strange and peculiar" conduct. He said, "It is not evidence of a crime, but it's not the conduct of your average citizen." There were other legal avenues available to pursue, and Bindner settled on defamation.

That case eventually went to nonbinding arbitration in which the City of Fairfield was recommended to pay Bindner $50,000. The city attorneys refused to pay and said they would take their chances in civil court. But two years later, right before the case was to go to trial, they settled for $90,000 (over $177,000 in 2025). Fairfield admitted no blame in agreeing to the settlement. Bindner's attorney said, "You don't pay $90,000 unless you've done something wrong. The officer's conduct was wrong and the statements they made were improper."

The Bindner pursuit fizzled.

New hope was ignited in 2023 when a former pastor, eighty-three-year-old David Zandstra, told investigators that he killed eight-year-old Gretchen Harrington in 1975 while she was walking to Bible camp in Pennsylvania. Doing some legwork, it was discovered that Zandstra had worked at the Christian Reformed Church in Fairfield from 1990 to 2005 and was in the city at the time of Campbell's alleged kidnapping.

Unfortunately, no link was found between Zandstra and the disappearance of Amanda Nikki Campbell. After more than three decades, the case remains open.

PRISCILLA STROLE—TECHNOLOGY CATCHES A KILLER

The March 11, 2019 episode of the HBO Max series *Betrayal* features a dramatization of the tragic events surrounding the murder of Fairfield resident Priscilla Strole. It is titled "Welcome to the Murderhood."

Priscilla Strole moved to Fairfield from the Bay Area with her teenage son Kyle Stracner to get a fresh start and get away from past abusive relationships.

On August 31, 1985, Kyle returned home around 9:45 p.m. after hanging out with friends. He knocked on the door but there was no answer. When he looked through a window, he saw the nude body of his mother on the floor and entered the house by climbing in through an unlocked window. When Kyle got a closer look at his mother, he ran screaming out the front door and the Fairfield Police Department was called.

Top: Priscilla Strole, who was brutally murdered in her Fairfield home. *Public domain.*

Bottom: Robert Hathaway's mug shot. He killed himself after DNA proved he killed Priscilla Strole. *Public domain.*

Priscilla Strole had been raped, beaten with a decorative piece of wood and stabbed in the face with a can opener and a knife. Detectives ruled out a random attack because it appeared she had known her rapist/killer.

There was no shortage of potential suspects. Strole had an abusive ex who was one of the reasons she had moved to Fairfield in the first place. Her across-the-street Fairfield neighbor seemed to have a thing for her and was always hanging out at her house, sometimes making her uncomfortable. Strole had had an affair with a married man, and the scorned wife snuck into their love den, stole their clothes and returned them, shredded, to her soon-to-be ex-husband's house.

But none of the leads panned out, as each potential suspect was cleared.

The case was stalled for twenty-nine years before it was revived by cold case detectives who reexamined the evidence. They started with DNA tests, but they came back with nothing. Then they realized that back in 1983 the federal Automated Fingerprint Identification System, which continually checks fingerprints, was not around yet. When they entered fingerprints found at the scene, they got a match.

The matching prints belonged to Kyle's then seventeen-year-old friend Robert Hathaway. He still lived in Fairfield, and in February 2014, detectives got a warrant to collect his DNA. They also questioned Hathaway, who was visibly nervous and sweating during the interview.

Four days later, Robert Hathaway died by suicide, leaving a note that said he was "taking the coward's way out." Although Kyle Stracner had died years earlier, Strole's older children had a measure of relief knowing who had killed their mother.

Erica Brown—Case Solved, But Still Missing

For centuries, there was a misconception that if there was no dead body, you could not convict someone of murder. The practice dates back to a 1660 case in England when a man vanished, and three individuals were hanged for his murder. Two years later, the missing man turned up alive after having been abducted and enslaved in Turkey.

Forensics has changed that notion of "no body, no crime." A recent example of this was the case of thirty-six-year-old Fairfield resident Erica Brown's murder.

On August 25, 2023, Brown went missing from her home. Police were immediately suspicious of the circumstances and within eleven days issued an arrest warrant for Erica Brown's boyfriend Mark Randle. The suspect was on the run for several weeks but was apprehended in September and charged with first-degree murder.

Randle's trial began on July 10, 2024. It was a clinic on how to construct a prosecutable case based solely on circumstantial evidence.

Key evidence came from two stolen vehicles linked to Randle. The first was a Chevy Malibu found burned out in Richmond. The second was a Mercedes found abandoned in Vallejo. Erica Brown's DNA and blood were collected from the burnt Chevy. The Mercedes had Randle's fingerprints and three empty but recently used gas cans in the trunk.

Jan Agacinski, Randle's mistress, tied the evidence together in court. On the night that Erica Brown went missing, Randle called Agacinski and she came over to his house. She saw Brown on a mattress in a bedroom. Brown was nude, unconscious and had obvious signs of trauma to her face and head.

Randle blamed Brown and said they had gotten into a fight because he had assumed she was cheating on him. Randle also said that in addition to beating Brown he'd waterboarded her. Agacinski left, and when she came back hours later, Randle told her that Brown was dead.

Instead of calling 911, Agacinski helped Randle dispose of Brown's body.

Erica Brown, who was murdered by Mark Randle in 2023. Her body has not been recovered. *Public domain.*

Jan Agacinski was charged with accessory after the fact but was granted immunity in exchange for testifying against Randle. Her testimony was backed up by other evidence. Agacinski said that they prepared the Chevy Malibu's trunk to load Brown's body into it by moving a blue tote. Prosecutors then played a recording of a neighbor's Ring doorbell camera that captured the pair moving the blue tote.

Agacinski testified that Brown's body had been leaning against one of the doors on the Malibu, and investigators found her blood in that exact location.

On July 25, 2024, after the jury deliberated for five hours, they found Mark Randle guilty. He was sentenced to twenty-five years to life in prison.

There was a measure of justice for the friends and family of Erica Brown, who was described as a hard worker and a sweet person who was always smiling.

Her body has still not been found.

The following are some open Fairfield cold cases:

MARCELLA WOOLSEY—Fairfield police found forty-year-old Marcella Margaret Woolsey on the kitchen floor of her home on Cedarbrook Drive on June 10, 1981. An anonymous caller tipped them off. The same anonymous caller contacted Intercommunity Hospital, which then called Solano Ambulance. Woolsey had been shot in the head with a small-caliber gun.

REGINALD INFANTE, who was fourteen years old, went to watch a softball game at Laurel Creek Park on June 12, 1998. He was struck by gunfire from a passing car on Tanglewood Drive and died the following day. The suspect's car was described as a dark blue or black 1992 Honda Prelude with dark-tinted windows and chrome trim all around. The car appeared to have been lowered and may have been modified for racing.

RALPH CLARENCE MOORE—On February 20, 2002, Martha Moore returned to her Broadway Street home after work and found her seventy-three-year-old husband, Ralph, on the dining room floor bleeding profusely

Ralph Moore, whose 2002 murder remains unsolved. *Public domain.*

from the head. Ralph Moore was a former planning commissioner for the city of Fairfield and was routinely referred to as a kind and giving man. He died eight days after the attack.

Ryan Lumagui was killed on July 10, 2005, on eastbound Interstate 80 at the Airbase Parkway offramp. His red 1994 Cadillac was fired on by the driver of a silver four-door sedan. Lumagui's car clipped the silver sedan and then veered right, crossing the Air Base Parkway off-ramp and heading down an embankment. He died of a gunshot wound in the upper body.

Office of the Governor

ARNOLD SCHWARZENEGGER
THE PEOPLE'S GOVERNOR

PROCLAMATION

11/11/2005

Governor Schwarzenegger Offers Reward for Information in the Murder of Ryan Lumagui

PROCLAMATION
by the
Governor of the State of California

WHEREAS, on July 10, 2005, a silver, compact-sized car pulled alongside 20-year-old Ryan Lumagui and the occupants fired gunshots at him as he drove eastbound on Interstate 80 in Fairfield, killing him; and WHEREAS, the Fairfield Police Department has pursued and exhausted all investigative leads and to date Ryan's murder remains unsolved; and WHEREAS, Fairfield Police Chief William R. Gresham has asked that a state reward be offered to encourage individuals with information about this crime to contact law enforcement; and WHEREAS, the family of Ryan Lumagui fully supports the reward; and WHEREAS, public awareness and assistance is vital to law enforcement, and rewards often encourage public cooperation essential to apprehend those who have committed serious offenses; and WHEREAS, the Governor is authorized by Penal Code section 1547(a) to offer rewards for information leading to the arrest and conviction of any person who has committed, or is charged with the commission of, an offense punishable by death; and WHEREAS, the reward will be paid in accordance with Penal Code section 1547. NOW, THEREFORE, I, ARNOLD SCHWARZENEGGER, Governor of the State of California, do hereby offer, effective immediately, a reward in the amount of $50,000 for new information, voluntarily given hereafter, leading to the arrest and conviction in a California court of the person or persons who committed or is/are charged with the commission of an offense punishable by death for the murder of Ryan Lumagui.
IN WITNESS WHEREOF I have here unto set my hand and caused the Great Seal of the State of California to be affixed this the eleventh day of November 2005. /s/ Arnold Schwarzenegger Governor of California

A reward announcement from Governor Arnold Schwarzeneggar for information on the murder of Ryan Lumagui. *Public domain.*

Phuong Le was reported missing April 25, 2010, after having last been seen at the coffee shop in the Barnes & Noble bookstore at 1600 Gateway Boulevard. Her body was found on May 15, 2010, along Highway 121 in Napa County. Le had immigrated to the United States from Vietnam when she was nine years old and had just completed a nursing program at Solano Community College.

Phuong Le, whose body was found in 2010. Her case remains unsolved. *Public domain.*

If you have any information to aid investigators in solving these or other crimes, contact the Solano County District Attorney's Cold Case Investigators' hotline at (707) 784-8477.

5

PROMINENT FAIRFIELD CRIME STORIES, PART 2

1957: Rose Ann White—An Unthinkable Murder

In *A Criminal History of Mankind*, author Colin Wilson explores the concept of so-called motiveless murder:

> *As I leafed my way through* True Detective, *I became aware of the emergence of a disturbing new trend: the completely pointless or "motiveless" murder. As long ago as 1912, André Gide had coined the term "gratuitous act: to describe this type of crime; the hero of his novel* Les Caves du Vatican *(which was translated as* Lafcadio's Adventures*) suddenly has the impulse to kill a total stranger on a train. "Who would know? A crime without a motive—what a puzzle for the police." So he opens the door and pushes the man to his death. Gide's novel was a black comedy; the "motiveless murder" was intended as a joke in the spirit of Oscar Wilde's essay about the loiterer who murdered his sister-in-law because she had thick ankles. Neither philosophers nor policemen seriously believed that such things were possible. Yet by 1959 it was happening.*

Actually, in Solano County, it happened two years earlier.

A January 7, 1957 *Solano Republican* newspaper all-caps-across-five-column-lengths-headline screamed, "Suisun City Girl Slain."

Described as "the most vicious crime in Solano County," the story was ghastly and tragic.

A fourteen-year-old Fairfield eighth-grade student, Roger Neal, was booked into Solano County juvenile hall on charges he murdered eight-year-old Rose Ann White of Suisun City the previous Saturday at dusk.

White was reported missing at 8:30 p.m. by her mother. At approximately 10:00 p.m., Fairfield Police Chief Rex Clift, who was assisting with the case, picked up Neal because Mrs. White said he'd been at her home that day.

Neal said he'd seen White earlier at the Crystal School playground. Clift continued to question him until 1:00 a.m. without further results. Fairfield Police Officer K.B. Thurston then questioned Neal until shortly before 3:00 a.m.

The boy admitted being with the girl near the Southern Pacific company right-of-way and said she'd fallen and injured herself. He then led investigators to the general area and showed them a rock, which he said White fell against and cut her head. A twenty-minute search of the area revealed the girl's body hidden face down under a pile of weeds.

Neal admitted that he had hit the girl on the head with a rock, stabbed her with a penknife and strangled her with a tetherball rope.

Sheriff Thomas E. Joyce said that autopsy reports showed the girl died of 7 stab wounds to the heart, 4 of them completely through the vital organ. There were a total of 123 stab wounds, 8 of them on the back and 115 on the chest and upper abdomen.

White had been hit on the head with the rock three times, a skull fracture being inflicted each time. Neal dragged her body halfway up a railroad bank, laid her on her back and stabbed her numerous times. Then he turned her over on her stomach and continued the relentless stabbing attack on her back. Neal knotted a tetherball rope around White's neck, covered her with brush and then went home.

Back at his house, he worked on his stamp collection, ate dinner with his mother and stepfather, showered, watched television and went to bed at 9:00 p.m.

Despite Rose Ann's panties being removed and buried some distance from the body, a detailed autopsy report showed the girl had not been "attacked" (evidently sexually). Neal said he removed them because he had gotten his fingerprints on them turning her over.

Officers said the youth showed no emotion during the night of questioning and searching for his alleged victim. The first display of emotion came after he was lodged in the county juvenile quarters in Vallejo. He cried for a few minutes.

"I don't know why I did it. I just did," Neal said. "I saw all those stabbings in the movies and on television and I wanted to find out what it was like."

On the way from jail to court for his arraignment on a murder charge, Neal told Sheriff's Deputy Hale Humphrey (whose own murder is detailed in the "Officer Down!" chapter) that he had recalled an "Oriental" method of execution by multiple stabs or cuts. He said he heard about it in Japan, where his stepfather was stationed as an anti-aircraftsman.

There were attempts to make sense of the tragedy, and Rex Clift said that Neal expressed hostility toward girls in general and to his twelve-year-old sister in particular because he felt that she got all the attention at home.

That theory was shot down by his stepfather and mother.

Rose Ann White's mother expressed sympathy for Roger's parents and felt that he was sick and needed to be in a mental institution.

Rose Ann White is buried in the Babyland section of the Suisun-Fairfield Cemetery on Union Avenue in Fairfield.

MURDER SCENE—Roger Brown, 14, of Fairfield, points to tetherball at scene of slaying of Rose Ann White, 8-year-old Suisun schoolgirl, as officers look on

Opposite: Suisun City resident Rose Ann White, who was killed by a fourteen-year-old playmate in 1957. *Fairfield Civic Center Library microfilm.*

Right: Fourteen-year-old Fairfield killer Roger Neal showing police where he hid the body of eight-year-old Rose Ann White. *Fairfield Civic Center Library microfilm.*

1961: Henry Shriver Shoots Wife for Bad Housekeeping

Here's a thought experiment: Can a husband ever be justified in trying to express his displeasure with his wife's housekeeping habits by threatening her with a shotgun? What if the shotgun then "accidentally" goes off and kills her? Well, it's not just a thought experiment. That's what happened on February 9, 1961, in Pleasants Valley in Vacaville.

Henry Shriver, a forty-year-old mechanic at Mare Island in Vallejo, had a few drinks at a bar on his way home from work that day. When he arrived at his house, he began arguing with his wife, Flora. The main bone of contention was that Henry felt she was "the world's worst housekeeper" and just sat around the house all day watching television and smoking cigarettes while dirty dishes and soiled laundry accumulated. Henry was also upset that their sixteen-year-old son had dropped out of school five weeks earlier and he had just found out about it, while his wife not only knew but also condoned it.

As he later explained to the district attorney, Henry Shriver took a single-barrel, 16-gauge shotgun off a rack on his wall and pointed it at his wife just to add an exclamation point to his insistence that she "righten" her ways. He contended that the shotgun just went off, killing Flora.

The couple's youngest children, ages six and seven, were asleep in the house but did not wake from the blast. The oldest son, who had dropped out

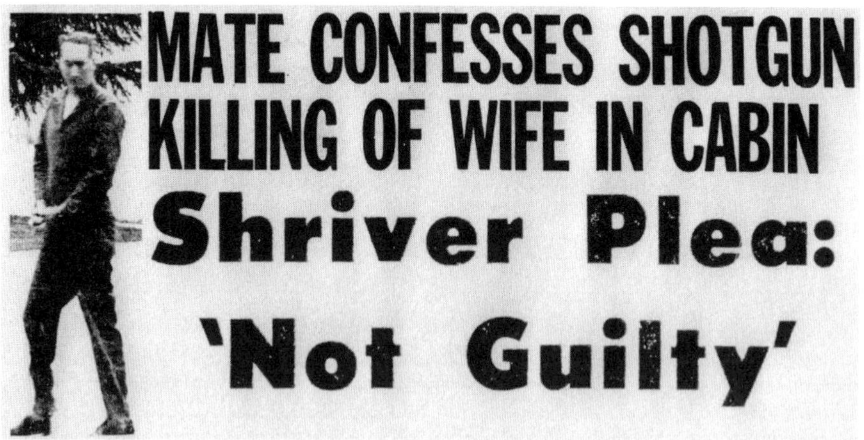
MATE CONFESSES SHOTGUN KILLING OF WIFE IN CABIN

Shriver Plea: 'Not Guilty'

Henry Shriver picture and headlines about his murder case in 1961. *Fairfield Civic Center Library microfilm.*

of school, was in the kitchen and said that he heard his mom say, "Please don't shoot me" right before she was killed. The Shrivers' fourteen-year-old daughter was outside and heard the fatal shot.

After the shooting, Shriver walked to a neighbor's house and called a doctor and the police.

The Shrivers had lived on their fifty-two-acre ranch, where they raised apricots and plums, since 1954. Sheriff Thomas Joyce said their house (described by some reporters as a very rustic cabin) was in a deplorable state of untidiness and called it "a squalid shack set atop a knoll." Joyce and his deputies had to walk nearly a quarter mile from the main road along a muddy roadway to reach it.

Because of the road conditions, officers had to borrow a tractor and wagon from a neighbor to bring Flora Shriver's three-hundred-pound body down to the waiting ambulance for transport to the Vacaville mortuary. Henry Shriver was charged with first-degree murder.

Shriver was arraigned in Vacaville, and then his case was bound over for trial in the Superior Court in Fairfield. The trial started in May 1961, and the district attorney asserted that Shriver planned to kill not only his wife but also his oldest son and then himself. Shriver claimed that the hammer on the rifle slipped forward as he was putting it away because it had no safety catch on it. A witness for the prosecution, an agent from the state criminal identification bureau, was at the trial just to testify that the gun in evidence was the murder weapon. But on cross-examination, he inadvertently scored a point for the defense. The agent demonstrated that it was possible for a person's finger to slip off the hammer so the gun could accidentally fire.

Henry Shriver's defense attorney called to the stand neighbors who testified to the truth of Flora's atrocious housekeeping. They said that she once brought a pig into the house and put it to bed. Other details included a bathtub filled with dirty laundry, the mess from seven un-housebroken cats and his wife letting one of their younger children eat from the same plate as a dog.

After the six-day trial, the jury found Henry Shriver guilty of manslaughter. The judge ordered a probation report, which would guide his decision for sentencing the following month.

Now, probation reports typically try to give an accurate rendering of the mitigating and aggravating factors to determine whether defendants are suitable candidates for probation or whether they should be incarcerated and for how long. One of the mitigating factors is whether or not the defendants showed remorse.

One way to not show remorse for what, in the most charitable light, was an accidental killing of your wife, is to get remarried five days after being found guilty of manslaughter. But that's exactly what Henry Shriver did.

He wed a waitress named Wanda Louise Davis. She actually had been living with Henry and Flora in January. During the trial, starting five days after the killing, Shriver and Davis had begun exchanging love letters. The new Mrs. Shriver was soon back living in the same filthy house where the former Mrs. Shriver had lived until she was shot.

In June 1961, Henry Shriver was denied probation and sentenced from one to ten years in the penitentiary. The probation report said, "Despite the positive aspects of Shriver's character, such as his record as an employee at Mare Island, we feel that his violent temper, lack of remorse and the ill-advised marriage would indicate he is unsuitable for an alternative to a prison sentence."

The report also questioned the defense used by Shriver at the trial that Flora was such a poor housekeeper that he at least had a right to frighten her with a loaded firearm. It went on to say that while the defendant's assertion about his wife's housekeeping was accurate, they had observed that the grounds outside the house, which were Mr. Shriver's responsibility, were just as deplorable as the interior.

The Shriver story has a rather odd postscript: In July 1961, a month after Shriver was sentenced and was still being processed at the California Medical Facility (CMF) in Vacaville, a twenty-acre brush fire broke out at the Shriver place. Harold Harrington, a friend of Henry's new wife, stopped by the house to cheer her up by playing his banjo. While he was there, he agreed to chop up some of the car hulks that belonged to Henry Shriver so Wanda could sell the scrap metal for money.

He was using an acetylene torch that set fire to the tall, dry brush growing all around the car parts. It took eight rigs and thirty firefighters to extinguish the blaze. Harrington was arrested for negligently starting the fire.

But wait, there's more.

The banjo that Harrington had brought to serenade Wanda Shriver? It had been stolen in Humboldt County.

Finally, if there was such a thing as the Pun Police, newspaper editors all over the state could have been charged with Assault with a Corny Headline for publishing that Harrington had to "face the music" for his crimes.

1967: The Abortion Trial of Dr. Felix Rossi Jr.

Dr. Felix Rafael Rossi Jr. started practicing medicine in Fairfield in the late 1930s and worked there for forty years. He was the family physician for numerous Fairfielders, many of whom he delivered as babies. They recall his kind disposition and the fact that he made house calls.

Dr. Rossi was a well-respected member of the community. In addition to belonging to several civic entities, he was instrumental in getting the Fairfield Hospital on Empire Street built. In 1951, when the Green Valley Country Club christened their new golf course, Dr. Rossi was given the honor of being the first member to tee off using a ceremonial gold golf ball.

In 1967, many Fairfield residents were shocked when a grand jury indicted Dr. Rossi on four counts of illegal abortion and four counts of sex perversion. The indictment charged the doctor with causing the miscarriages of four women and performing a perverted act on two of them. The abortion case and sex perversion cases were tried separately so the latter charges would not prejudice jurors making their decision on the former ones.

The penalty for abortion was a two-to-five-year prison sentence. Because of his status in the community, a succession of judges who were personal friends of Rossi had to recuse themselves and an Alameda County judge presided over the case.

The abortion trial started in July 1967, and the district attorney said that Rossi had routinely performed illegal abortions. The average cost for them was $300 to $500 (approximately $2,800 to $4,600 in 2025). The prosecution tried to score points with the jury by pointing out that the patients came to Dr. Rossi's office at night and some came to the back door of the hospital. The defense countered that the reason for the furtive arrivals was because the women were unmarried and pregnant and did not want to be seen.

The trial lasted two weeks, and halfway through it, the judge dismissed three of the four charges, as he ruled the prosecution failed to produce evidence beyond the testimony of the complainants.

OVER 120,000 READERS
THE NEWSPAPER THAT GOES INTO ALL THE HOMES EVERY MORNING

Vallejo Times-Herald
SOLANO AND NAPA COUNTY'S MORNING NEWSPAPER

CONTINUED CLEAR

92ND YEAR—No. 320 VALLEJO, CALIF.—MARE ISLAND—HQ. S.F. BAY NAVAL SHIPYARD—FRIDAY, JULY 21, 1967 FOUR SECTIONS—32 PAGES

JURY ACQUITS DR. ROSSI!

Headline about Dr. Rossi's acquittal in his abortion trial. *Newspapers.com.*

The one remaining charge focused on a claim by a nineteen-year-old Sacramento State student. She testified that Dr. Rossi had performed an abortion for her and charged her $300, but there were complications. Dr. Rossi returned the money plus an extra $200 for the young lady and her boyfriend. The district attorney framed the reason for the refund as "to keep their mouths shut."

Dr. Rossi testified that he examined the woman to give her medical options and suggest courses of treatment. He discovered the fetus was partially naturally aborted and advised the woman to seek a doctor near her school.

On July 20, 1967, after deliberating for five hours, the jury reached a unanimous verdict of not guilty. When the verdict was read, members of the audience who had sat through the trial applauded.

But Dr. Rossi was not out of the woods completely. He still had to face the sex perversion charges. Two women, one from Vallejo and one from Vacaville, were the complainants in that case. He was acquitted.

Then in October 1972, a $200,000 civil suit was filed in Solano Superior Court against Dr. Rossi. The woman who initiated the suit claimed Dr. Rossi drugged her and committed "an unnatural sex act" with her against her will when she came to him in July of that year for a weight problem.

In August 1973, Dr. Rossi fired back by filing a $3,000 invasion of privacy suit against the woman who had sued him. It was for the patient concealing a tape recorder in her purse and recording their conversation.

The cases were settled out of court for undisclosed sums. Dr. Felix Rossi died in 2008.

1968: The Police Shooting of Jose Alvarado

Police body cameras have become a standard in many municipalities in the United States, which has eliminated the need to rely exclusively on witness testimony. In 1968, however, the technology for affordable body cams did not yet exist and so the case of Jose Alvarado still has unanswered questions decades later.

The facts are that on Sunday, September 8, 1968, Fairfield police were dispatched to 924 Johnson Street. One of Alvarado's sons had called to report that his father was fighting with his mother. Two patrolmen arrived at the scene and encountered Alvarado, who was wielding a meat cleaver. Two other officers were dispatched to assist the first pair.

Fairfield Police Chief Vern Coppock reported that the first two officers tried to calm Alvarado, but he threatened them with the cleaver and chased them around a car. Alvarado's first swing drove the weapon into the police car. His second swing missed his target and hit the garage wall. When the other two officers arrived, they attempted to subdue Alvarado with mace, but it was ineffective.

Jose Alvarado wielding a meat cleaver moments before he was shot and killed by a Fairfield police officer. *Newspapers.com.*

When Sergeant David Huff arrived at the scene, his assessment was that Alvarado was about to throw the meat cleaver. Since they were under orders not to place themselves in a position to be maimed or killed, Huff shot Alvarado in the chest from about twenty feet away. According to reports, about thirty-five people witnessed the shooting. Most of them were children.

Alvarado was taken to the Solano County Hospital, where he died in surgery.

The police spoke to and recorded the statements of several witnesses who verified the police account. However, there were some who contradicted it.

Across-the-street neighbor Dick Ross said that "those four policemen had sprayed him with mace and he was down on the ground in shock and unable to see. They could have walked over and taken the cleaver. This sergeant pulls in, gets out and shoots him. He was trying to give up. All the neighbors saw it. I don't understand why they're not talking."

The controversy was ignited; it smoldered and then burst into flames.

Three days later, almost one hundred people protested the shooting by marching in front of city hall and the police station. Many of them were members of the Solano Mexican-American Committee for Justice, which formed after the incident, and others were members of the Mexican-American Political Association (MAPA).

Some of the signs they carried read "Police Brutality Will Not Be Tolerated," "Murder Is Not Law and Order," and "The Alvarado Family Wants Justice." A spokesperson for the Solano Mexican-American Committee for Justice called for a third-party investigation and suspension of Sergeant Huff. The chairman of the group sent letters to the U.S. attorney and the California attorney general that read in part: "We, the United Mexicans for Justice, demand that an impartial investigation take place by your department only to prove to the world what we already knew: that the police of Fairfield are racist and that justice that is in the books does not extend to the Mexican."

The FBI conducted a brief investigation and submitted a report to the Justice Department. The department wanted more facts to see if a full investigation was warranted. Since a full investigation was not announced, evidently the facts did not call for it.

The autopsy on Alvarado revealed that his blood alcohol level was .20. Authorities in 1968 considered .10 sufficient to charge a man as drunk (now it is .08). That would help explain why the mace was ineffective.

A front-page article in the *San Francisco Examiner* added details that local coverage did not. Earlier that day, Jose Alvarado had started drinking and was getting depressed and sat alone in the living room with a .22 rifle.

Fairfield Mexican Americans protesting the police shooting of Jose Alvarado in 1968. *Fairfield Civic Center Library microfilm.*

His wife, Tommie Alvarado, was able to grab the rifle and take it across the street to neighbors. She questioned why she, a woman who was seven months pregnant, could do that but four trained officers could not handle her husband. According to the piece, when Alvarado was hit with the mace he tried to wipe it from his eyes with a piece of canvas on his driveway and with a plant he ripped from the lawn and rubbed on his face. After he was shot, Tommie Alvarado ran to her fallen husband and kissed him. Her lips were burned by the mace.

Sergeant Huff's attorney sent a letter to the *Examiner* protesting that the tenor of the article inferred that Alvarado's death was unjustifiably caused by Huff. The *Examiner* responded with a correction and clarification statement basically saying their intent was to report on the incident and retracted a phrase used by a witness: "in all but cold blood."

Predictably, lawsuits followed.

Sergeant Huff filed a $1 million lawsuit against the *San Francisco Examiner* and several individuals involved in the story. Then in October, he filed a $5 million slander and libel suit against MAPA and others who alleged that he had previously pistol-whipped a man. Others named were Dick Ross, who accused Huff of "an act of cold-blooded murder." One detail that the suit included was that following an incident that involved a weapon in 1965, Tommie Alvarado had petitioned to have her husband committed to Napa State Hospital as an insane person.

In October, Tommie Alvarado filed a $1 million wrongful death lawsuit against Sergeant Huff and the City of Fairfield.

Fairfield City Manager B. Gale Wilson announced in January 1970 that Sergeant David Huff had been fired for insubordination and failure to obey a lawful order for a different incident. Huff had been suspended earlier that month following an investigation of a citizen's complaint against him that was described in press reports only as "of a serious nature."

In the process of the investigation, Huff was ordered to take a polygraph (lie detector) test, and on the advice of his counsel, he refused. Wilson said that the city had clear statutory authority to require use of the polygraph and officers were required to cooperate. He went on to stress that the firing had absolutely nothing to do with the earlier Alvarado shooting.

In April 1973, after a two-week trial, then former Fairfield Police Officer Huff was exonerated by a 9–3 verdict in the $1 million wrongful death suit brought by Tommie Alvarado.

1972: The Trial of Serial Killer Juan Corona

When Juan Vallejo Corona was convicted of the grisly murders of twenty-five itinerant farmworkers in 1973, he was known as the worst mass murderer in U.S. history.

His horrifying record was surpassed by serial killer John Wayne Gacy in 1980.

The shocking saga began on May 19, 1971, when Yuba City rancher Goro Kagehiro discovered a deep hole on his property. Returning that night, he saw that it was filled in. The next day, Kagehiro called the sheriff, expecting that someone had illegally buried trash in his peach orchard.

Instead of the expected trash, the body of forty-year-old transient laborer Kenneth Whitacre was found. He had been stabbed in the chest, bashed in the skull and slashed across the back of his head.

Four days later, workers at the nearby Sullivan Ranch found another buried body. Then another. And another. Eventually, twenty-five bodies were discovered and twenty-one of them identified. All of the men had been bludgeoned and stabbed, and one was also shot. They were buried face-up with their arms extended over their heads and their shirts over their faces, which had been mutilated with a machete. Many of them had no pants on or the pants were around their ankles.

Juan Corona, a successful and well-liked labor contractor with a family, was not the obvious suspect. As with most crimes, it was the evidence that pointed the finger of blame his way. The evidence against Corona was circumstantial, but compelling. Meat receipts with his signature were found in one grave, and bank deposit slips with his name and address on them were in two others. Some of the victims had also last been seen in his truck, according to witnesses.

A search of Corona's house yielded a machete, two bloodstained knives, a pistol of the same caliber as one used on the lone gunshot victim, bloodstained clothing and, most damning, a work ledger with thirty-four names and dates that included seven of the identified victims.

The prosecution at his trial later referred to it as Corona's "death list."

Corona reportedly had a reputation as a bit of a loose cannon coupled with a history of mental illness. The latter included an incident in 1955 when Corona had a schizophrenic episode where he believed he saw the ghosts of thirty-eight people who died in a levee-busting in Yuba City. The following year, Juan's half-brother Natividad Corona had him committed to Auburn's DeWitt State Hospital, where he was diagnosed with paranoid schizophrenia and given twenty-three electroshock treatments.

Corona was released three months later and, as he was in the United States illegally, was deported back to his native Mexico. He returned to the states legally soon afterward and in 1962 became a licensed labor contractor. Corona would scour seedy bars and hire desperate men, often alcoholics with no ties to any families called "fruit tramps," to work on ranches.

Serial killer Juan Corona at his trial in downtown Fairfield in 1972. *History of the Solano County Sheriff's Office Facebook page.*

Before killing, mutilating and burying his victims, Corona, a sexual sadist, sodomized them. His murderous rampage that claimed the lives of twenty-five people had taken place during a six-week period in 1971. His murder trial began in 1972.

His would not be a capital case because on February 18, 1972, the California Supreme Court ruled that the death penalty was unconstitutional.

Corona's defense attorney, Richard Hawk, was successful in getting a change of venue from Sutter County to Solano County because of pretrial publicity. The trial began on September 11, 1972, at Fairfield's courthouse.

Mexican American protestors encouraged by the defense picketed down Union Avenue with signs that said, among other things, "Don't Pick a Racist Jury," as the majority of the murder victims were Caucasian.

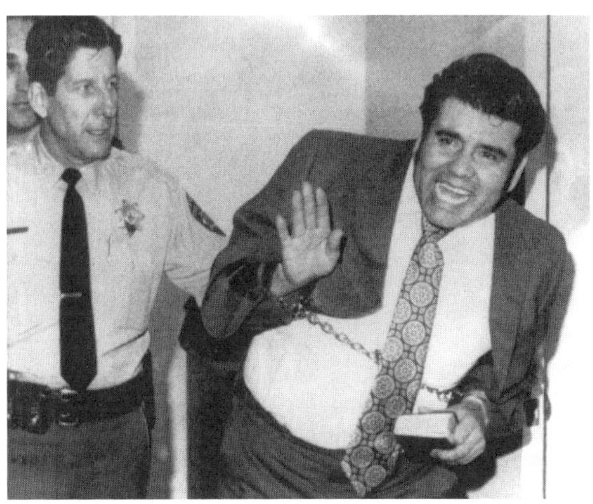

Handcuffed serial killer Juan Corona waves to family leaving his trial at the Fairfield courthouse. *History of the Solano County Sheriff's Office Facebook page.*

Corona's family were not fond of Sutter County District Attorney Dave Teja, who claimed one of Corona's sisters tried to push him down the courthouse stairs one day. According to Teja, the same sister tried to run him over with her car on another occasion.

Several prosecution blunders, including mislabeling evidence, almost derailed their case. Defense attorney Hawk claimed all along that there was no merit to the charges against his client, yet he rested his case without calling a single defense witness or having Corona testify on his own behalf.

After the end of the three-month trial, the jury deliberated for forty-five hours. Corona was found guilty on all twenty-five counts and sentenced to twenty-five consecutive terms of life imprisonment.

An appellate court overturned the conviction on May 18, 1978, citing Hawk's incompetence in not putting forward schizophrenia as a mitigating factor or having Corona plead insanity. Hawk was later cited for multiple counts of contempt and still later was disbarred for income tax evasion.

A second trial in Hayward began on February 22, 1982, and ended on September 23, 1982, with the same result.

Corona is sometimes seen as the forgotten serial killer because so many more infamous ones came after him. Part of the reason is that his victims were people who came from marginalized communities. But after Corona there was an explosion of serial killers that included Ted Bundy, Edmund Kemper, the Son of Sam, the Hillside Stranglers and the Golden State Killer.

In 1982, shortly after being convicted in the retrial, Corona was stabbed by a fellow inmate over thirty times with an X-ACTO knife, which resulted in the loss of his left eye.

In December 2011, Corona was nearly blind in his other eye and suffering from dementia at California State Prison, Corcoran. He had a parole hearing and, for the first time, confessed to the murderers. The reason he gave for killing the "fruit tramps"?

They were trespassing.

His parole was denied.

Juan Corona died on March 4, 2019, at the age of eighty-five.

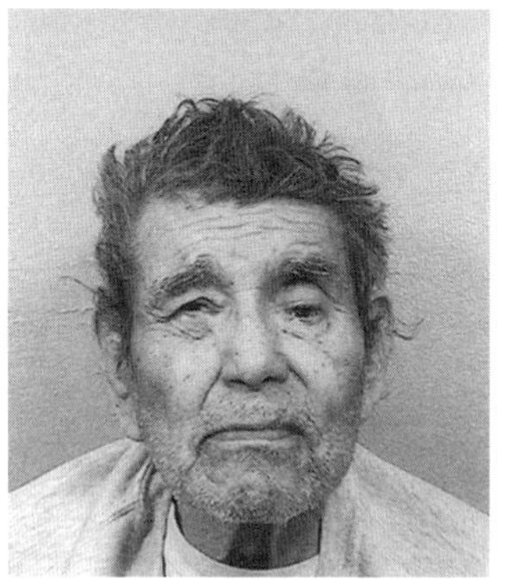

Juan Corona in 2018. *Public domain.*

1974: THE MORRIS MOTORS MURDERS

Many old-school Fairfielders recall local car dealers like Stan Motors or Chet Monez Ford, and usually the memories are pleasant, but recollections of Morris Motors are at best bittersweet.

Laurence D. "Larry" Morris Jr. was a graduate of St. Vincent's High School in Vallejo and attended Vallejo Junior College before serving two years in the army. In the service, he was a member of a precision drill team that performed all over the world. He came to Fairfield in 1959, was wed in 1963, and he and his wife, Jo Ann, had three children.

He opened Morris Motors in 1966 to sell dependable used cars at 2211 North Texas Street (later the site of Grand Auto and currently Goodwill). Unlike some of the more traditional advertisements for used cars at the time, Morris Motors' ads were a bit more unconventional. For example, this one from December 1967: "'WILD!' Morris Motors has gone wild on cutting prices due to the fact that we need some Christmas money!"

In 1970, the company expanded, adding a second lot at 2135 North Texas called Morris Motors & Trailer Sales, that specialized in travel trailers.

Larry Morris was enmeshed in the local community. He was active in the Moose Lodge and Native Sons of the Golden West, his company sponsored a local softball team and he was the 1965 campaign chairman for the Fairfield-Suisun American Cancer Society.

Professionally, Morris was honored at the National Independent Auto Dealers Association in Houston, Texas, in early March 1974. The group, composed of independent non-franchised auto dealers, elected him as their national secretary.

It was a post Morris held for about one week.

On March 14, 1974, at about 2:30 p.m., nineteen-year-old Fairfield resident Ronald Echols got into an argument with twenty-one-year-old Morris Motors lot attendant Carl Ley. The dispute was about repairs to a red 1969 Buick convertible Echols had purchased a few months earlier. The argument escalated, and Echols shot Ley five times in the face at point-blank range with a .22-caliber automatic rifle.

Larry Morris, who was in the office, came out when the shooting began and was shot in the head. He received emergency treatment at Intercommunity Hospital before being transferred to Queen of the Valley Hospital in Napa for neurosurgery. He died there about two hours after the shooting.

A description of Echols and his car was given to authorities by witnesses, and an all-points bulletin went out.

Today's Market

NEW YORK (UPI) — Stocks opened strong today but turned mixed near the close in active trading.

The Dow Jones industrial average lost 1.86 to 889.78. Shortly before the close Stan

(Please turn to page 6)

The Daily Republic

Successor to the Solano Republican

Serving Upper Solano County—The Fairfield-Vacaville-Suisun-Travis Area

SPECIAL: 2nd EDITION
FAIRFIELD HOMICIDE

HOME OF TRAVIS AIR FORCE BASE — THURSDAY, MARCH 14, 1974

Double Shooting Leaves Two Dead

Local Auto Dealer, Lotman Dead

FAIRFIELD—One man is dead and another receiving emergency treatment for a gunshot wound following a shooting today in a local used car lot.

Carl Lay, 21, of Fairfield, was shot five times and killed at about 2:30 p.m. today in the Morris Motors used car lot at 2135 N. Texas St. when a young man armed with a .22 caliber pistol became involved in an argument with lot owner Larry Morris, 38, of Fairfield.

Morris, also shot by the gunman, was transported to Intercommunity Memorial Hospital. He was later transferred by ambulance to Queen of the Valley Hospital in Napa for emergency neurosurgery. Morris reportedly sustained one bullet wound to the head.

Police reportedly are looking for a young Black man wearing a green field jacket and knit cap. The suspected gunman was reportedly driving a black and red 1969 convertible, and was last seen traveling northbound on N. Texas St. here.

According to FPD Sgt. J.L. Newcomb, the identity of the gunman may be known to law enforcement authorities.

"We have an idea now who might be responsible for this," Newcomb said.

A series of vehicle stops by Vacaville and Fairfield Police and California Highway Patrolmen immediately after the shooting failed to turn up the suspect.

A witness to the shooting, believed to be driving an orange American Motors AMX sports car with Texas license plates, also is being sought by authorities.

Laurence D. Morris Jr. came to Fairfield in 1969 as manager of the Beneficial Finance Company.

The son of Mr. and Mrs. Laurence D. Morris, Sr. of Vallejo, he was graduated from St. Vincent's High School in Vallejo and attended Vallejo Junior College before serving two years with the Army.

Laurence D. Morris Jr.

Bulletin

NAPA—Local auto dealer Larry Morris died here today at Queen of the Valley Hospital approximately two hours after he was shot in the head, according to hospital spokesman here.

Married in Holy Spirit Catholic Church in Fairfield in 1963 to the former Jo Ann L. Johnston, of Roseville, he resided at 1917 Fairfield Ave. here with his wife and adopted son, Scottie, age 4. Two married daughters by a previous marriage, Tana and Sandy, were former employees of The Daily Republic.

A long-time Trade Club member, he served last year as Head Trader for the Fairfield Club.

LAW ENFORCEMENT OFFICIALS, including Fairfield policemen, investigate the scene of this afternoon's double shooting and homicide at Morris Motors, 2135 N. Texas St.—DR Photo by Richter

The *Daily Republic* front page after the 1974 Morris Motors murders. *Fairfield Civic Center Library microfilm.*

The next morning, the red Buick convertible was found abandoned near Solano Community College, and shortly afterward a man fitting Echols's description was spotted walking near the Willotta Oaks area off Rockville Road. He had ditched his car and hitched a ride to the Iwama Market.

Police speculated that one of the reasons Echols was unable to make a clean getaway had to do with a fact of life in 1974: odd-even gas rationing. March 14 was an even-numbered day, and his license plate number ended in an odd digit, so he couldn't gas up his car and put some distance between himself and Fairfield.

At his arraignment, Echols would not give the judge his correct name, and a sanity hearing was set for late March to determine his fitness for trial. Echols had attended Crystal Intermediate School and Fairfield High School before joining the U.S. Marine Corps. He was discharged from the Marines for a "nervous condition."

Two psychiatrists testified for more than two hours, and the court found that Echols was sane and capable of cooperating with counsel in his defense. The public defender said that Echols was not responsive to questions about the case and that he rambled on about other subjects rather than answering questions.

At the trial, witnesses included a customer who was at Morris Motors at the time of the incident and a clerk at the Fairfield Kmart who testified he sold rifle shells to Echols before the shooting. The weapon used was never found. Another witness was a female friend of Echols who testified that he had confessed the crime to her.

It came out in the trial that Echols and Ley had known each other before the shooting. A former roommate of Echols named Mitch Gibson testified about an incident in Ley's apartment four days before the shooting when Ley picked up a machete to stop a fight between Echols and Gibson.

When given their opportunity, Echols's attorneys attempted to build a defense of diminished capacity. Echols's mother and two psychiatrists talked about his history of mental issues, including being discharged from the Marines. His mother testified that he had spent about four months in a naval hospital in San Diego and a month and a half in the Veterans Administration Hospital in Martinez due to mental issues.

IF YOU'RE IN THE MARKET for a top quality used automobile or a new travel trailer, Morris Motors and Trailer Sales is just the place to visit. Pictured above at their car lot are (left to right) Don Riddle, Joe Peterson, owner Larry Morris, and Gene Niman. DR photo by Robinson.

A 1971 Morris Motors ad in the *Daily Republic*. *Fairfield Civic Center Library microfilm.*

A psychiatrist from the California Medical Facility in Vacaville examined Echols and determined that he was probably suffering from paranoid schizophrenia at the time of the shooting and was unable to form the specific mental intent to commit murder because of his diminished capacity. A doctor from the Martinez VA Hospital said that Echols was not psychotic (unable to distinguish reality consistently) but had a paranoid personality characterized by suspiciousness, poor judgment and a tendency to blame others for his problems.

Following five days of testimony, the Superior Court jury deliberated for two days. On June 25, 1974, Echols was convicted of involuntary manslaughter. The penalty was one to fourteen years' imprisonment with parole eligibility after eighteen months. He was also convicted of being armed with and using a deadly weapon.

After a sanity hearing, Echols was determined to be not guilty by reason of insanity and committed to Atascadero State Hospital. In 1976, a new evaluation was ordered when the court received word that Echols had improved to the point that he was no longer a danger to the public. In 1979, he was moved to Napa State Hospital, was released to outpatient status in 1980 but was committed again the following year. In 1981, he got into a quarrel with another person and shot him (evidently not fatal) and said it was self-defense.

1983: The Armijo High Spy

If Armijo High School class of 1952 grad James Durward Harper had attended his twenty-fifth reunion in 1977, he would have had an unequaled success story to share with his classmates. The company he founded, Harper Time & Electronics, created the first digital stopwatch, priced at $200 (over $1,400 in 2025). Harper's company manufactured approximately 1,500 units per month and claimed to have captured more than 85 percent of the electronic digital stopwatch market.

James Harper would not have been able to attend his class's thirty-fifth reunion in 1987. That's because he was in his third year of a life sentence after having been convicted of espionage.

The Fairfield that James Harper grew up in was very different from today. Back in the late 1940s and early 1950s, it was a small, mainly agricultural town with slightly more than three thousand residents. Harper was remembered

Left: The Accusplit, the digital stopwatch that spy and Armijo grad James Harper invented. *Newspapers.com.*

Right: Convicted spy James Harper's Armijo High School senior picture. *1952 Armijo High School* La Mezcla *Yearbook.*

as kind of a quiet, moody guy who did not like to study but was a whiz at math and science. He was a decent halfback on the Armijo football team, but a knee injury in his senior year ended any dreams of future athletic glory.

While Harper was growing up, his parents separated, and while that is rather common these days, in the early 1950s small-town Fairfield it was not. A friend who knew Harper back then was quoted anonymously in the *Daily Republic* in 1984: "He had the typical problems a boy without a father has. When he went astray there was no one to kick him in the fanny. His value system was screwed up."

Harper enlisted in the U.S. Marine Corps after high school and was sent to electronics school at the naval base on Treasure Island in the San Francisco Bay. It was his first exposure to that kind of technology. By the early 1960s, he had arrived in what was later called Silicon Valley. After fits and starts with other projects like designing high-voltage power supplies, he and thirty-one co-investors started Harper Time & Electronics.

Harper reportedly had the idea to create a handheld stopwatch while watching his daughters race. His digital stopwatch was called Accusplit. Until Harper, no one had figured out how to make a battery-powered watch that used a tricky neon gas discharge display.

The company had problems, not the least of which was Harper himself, who reportedly "spent money like a drunken sailor." He also shaved his head, traded the then traditional three-piece suits for T-shirts and jeans and hung dozens of framed pictures of nude women on his wall's office next to diplomas and other decorations.

His heavy drinking also didn't endear him to his peers, and a year after he founded the company, he was fired by its board of directors. The company eventually went belly-up, and after bankruptcy, the patent rights to the digital stopwatch were included as part of the assets that were sold to a couple of entrepreneurs.

In the 1970s, Harper married his second wife, Ruby Schuler. She was the executive secretary to the president of a Palo Alto firm doing research for the Ballistic Missile Defense Advanced Technology Center in Huntsville, Alabama. Schuler had a mid-level "secret" security clearance. In hindsight, it seems surprising that she was given that level of clearance since she was known to be an alcoholic who had been arrested for drunk driving.

Armijo grad pleads guilty to espionage

SAN FRANCISCO (UPI) — Accused spy James D. Harper tried to plead guilty Friday to a single charge of espionage for selling Silicon Valley missile secrets to Soviet agents, but a federal judge refused to accept it.

Judge Samuel Conti told Harper to think about the seriousness of the charge during the weekend and return to court Monday.

Harper's guilty plea on the one count had been worked out with government lawyers.

The government's advantage in agreeing to the plea bargain would be that they had secrets that they did not want disclosed during a jury trial.

The list of documents Harper was charged with giving to the Soviet bloc agents was considered enormously valuable. They included missile secrets and documents dealing with America's ability to survive a nuclear attack.

A federal appeals court decision last week said Harper could not be sentenced to death if found guilty of espionage, paving the way for Friday's move by the accused spy's lawyer, Jerrold Ladar.

Attorneys for both sides refused to disclose any details of the plea bargain.

JAMES D. HARPER
Told to reconsider

"He could get anything from straight probation to life in prison," said Ladar.

Harper, 49, a free-lance engineer in the technology-rich Silicon Valley and a former Fairfield resident and Armijo High graduate, was charged with stealing Minuteman missile secrets and 58 other sensitive documents in 1979.

See Harper, Page 16a

Armijo High Class of 1952 grad and convicted spy James Durward Harper. *Fairfield Civic Center Library microfilm.*

There is speculation about Harper's motivation for becoming a spy. Money, adventure, whatever the reason, at some point he had the idea to try peddling phony U.S. defense secrets to Polish spies. A former colleague of Harper's, who was well aware of his friend's penchant for wild behavior and had nicknamed him "Crazy Jim," told Harper to stay away from spies or he could "end up dead or in jail."

Harper ignored that advice.

On October 15, 1983, the FBI arrested Harper, then forty-nine and working as a freelance electrical engineer in Mountain View. He was charged with selling Minuteman missile secrets to the Soviet Union.

The story of his arrest broke nationally and was printed in the October 18, 1983 *Daily Republic* with the headline "Bay Area Man Held in Sale of U.S. Secrets." It became clear within a few days that the spy identified initially just as a "Bay Area man" was from Fairfield.

Harper had copied classified documents in his wife's possession at night and on weekends, and from July 1979 to November 1981, he passed them on to Polish intelligence officials, who in turn passed them on to the Soviet

Union's security agency, the KGB. It is estimated that with the help of Ruby Schuler, Harper secretly photocopied around two hundred pounds of classified papers that he sold in the international espionage market.

Ruby Louise Schuler died of cirrhosis of the liver at age thirty-nine, four months before Harper's arrest.

Harper was paid $250,000 (close to $800,000 in 2025) for the national defense secrets he stole. The Soviet agents involved in procuring them were given commendations by then-KGB leader Yuri Andropov.

The information that Harper sold was not inconsequential. An FBI affidavit stated that it included extremely sensitive research by the Department of Defense concerning the ability of the United States' Minuteman missiles to survive a preemptive nuclear attack by the Soviet Union.

Whether he was motivated by twinges of conscience or a fear of prosecution is unclear, but in September 1981, two years before his arrest, Harper anonymously attempted to broker a deal for immunity with the CIA through an attorney. That offer was rejected, and Harper continued to sell secrets. He was later identified by a Polish double agent.

The effect of Harper's actions on the United States' national security were significant. A ballistic missiles expert who had advised the Joint Chiefs of Staff, the National Security Council and Congress said that the papers delivered by Harper "have done damage to the U.S. in several areas that can have a severe effect on our country and particularly ballistic missile research even into the 21st century."

James Durward Harper was sentenced to life in prison on May 14, 1984. Presiding Federal Judge Samuel Conti, who originally wanted to sentence him to death but was overruled by an appellate court, told Harper: "You are a traitor to your country who committed the crime not for any political reasons, but for greed."

Author's Note: In April 2014, I published a Back in the Day column about James Harper in the Fairfield Daily Republic. *I thought it would be fair to try to get his side of the story straight from the horse's mouth, so I sent him a letter to his "home" at Lompoc Federal Penitentiary. He wrote me back a little while later. His letter surprised me because instead of talking about the case (he only said that my column was wrong), he mainly mused about growing up in Fairfield and talked about going on hayrides and playing with neighborhood friends.*

I wrote back asking him to clarify what was wrong with my piece, but he never got back with me. In 2018, when I was going to follow up again, I learned that he had been released from prison two years prior at the age of eighty-two. In July 2019, I received an email from Harper, who was reaching out to me for help in finding his brother, whom he had not seen in decades. He included his phone number, so I called him and we spoke for a while. He was living in Arkansas with a woman who was a former classmate. I wanted to do a follow-up column on him, but life and the pandemic got in the way. When I finally tried contacting him again in 2022, I learned that he had died the week before.

1986: Aquarius and Lucky

Merriam Webster defines a head shop as "a shop specializing in articles (such as hashish pipes and roach clips) of interest to drug users." Now some may bristle at the rather blunt definition, as head shops often include so many more items. Fairfield had its share of them over the years. When Eucalyptus Records & Tapes moved to North Texas Street in the spot formerly occupied by Pinkerton's Hardware, part of the store could definitely be called a head shop. There was another, Imports International, located in the Solano Mall. But the head shop that most old-school Fairfielders recall was the Aquarius Gift Shop, located at 750 Texas Street.

Longtimers fondly remember all the marijuana paraphernalia and related items like bongs, *High Times* magazines and *The Fabulous Furry Freak Brothers* comic books, but it also carried items like magic tricks, puka shell necklaces, switchblade combs, strawberry oil perfume, Farrah Fawcett posters, macramé plant hangers and much more.

Many posted their recollections in Fairfield-themed Facebook groups:

> **Ellen Hornback:** I loved Aquarius! It was the coolest store in town for teens and young people. It was one-stop shopping for all our party needs! Remember the little black light room full of posters from floor to ceiling?
> **Bill Haynes:** I bought my first pack of Zig Zags and a bong there…shhhhh.
> **Jeff Johnson:** We bought every last poster for a buck each when it was closing down. I can still smell the mix of incense that blessed you as you walked in and the bells rang! Those were the best days!
> **Jack Burton:** They had everything from cinnamon toothpicks to whoopie cushions.
> **Sheri Sotomayor:** I worked there at age fifteen selling roach clips and had no idea what they were!

Aquarius Gift Shop

The Aquarius Gift Shop. *1973 Armijo High School* La Mezcla *Yearbook.*

In addition to the aforementioned items, Aquarius sold coins. The owner of Aquarius was Reuben Williams, who went by the nickname Lucky. He and his wife, Marie, who was originally from France, were both well-liked members of the community. In fact, Lucky was a member of fifteen numismatic societies, including being a founding member and past president of the Napa Numismatic Society. In the mid-1980s, Lucky closed the Fairfield location and opened the Golden Hills Coin Exchange on the 700 block of Merchant Street in Vacaville.

On Monday, November 3, 1986, Solano County morning newspapers reported that Lucky, a Fairfield resident, was missing and had not been seen since the previous Saturday at a 5:45 p.m. The next day, Lucky's body was found lying in a creek bed along Cherry Glen Road in Vacaville. He had been shot in the head twice.

Based on the evidence collected at the scene where his body was found and at the Golden Hills Coin Exchange, police were able to deduce that he had been robbed, killed and his body dumped in the creek bed. What they didn't have was a suspect, and Lucky's murder remained unsolved for years.

The break in the case came in July 1990 over 1,100 miles away in Billings, Montana. Police in big sky country were investigating the murder of a coin shop owner named Charles Sparboe who had been shot in the head along with a woman named Catherine Newstrom and robbed of $54,000 in coins and gold.

A Polaroid photo of Marie and Lucky Williams. *Joe Conception.*

Investigators in several states then compared notes and realized that they were not dealing with random, isolated crimes but with the work of a serial killer who was likely responsible for at least fifteen murders.

The killer's modus operandi was the same wherever he went: He would go to a coin shop and pretend to be a customer, often visiting several times. He was amiable and chatty but would return one more time to shoot the owner and steal thousands of dollars of merchandise.

Charles Thurman Sinclair, who had been using the alias J.C. Weir for at least five years, was arrested at his home in Kenny Lake, Alaska. Tracking him down involved some old-fashioned police work.

Days before his murder, Charles Sparboe had voiced to his son Jim concerns about the odd new customer who was hanging around his shop. After the body was found, Jim Sparboe provided a composite drawing of the suspect, and the Billings police sent it out via teletype. It triggered recognition in squad rooms in Everett, Washington; Mishawaka, Iowa; Spokane, Washington; and many more, including Vacaville, California.

While the considerable circumstantial evidence pointed to Sinclair, there was also a victim who survived an attack. On May 4, 1990, Kelly Finnegan was shot in the head with a small-caliber gun at his coin shop in Murray, Utah. Right before he was shot, Finnegan turned his head, which probably saved his life. The bullet pierced his forehead, but he was not seriously wounded. He fell to the floor and played dead while the would-be killer/robber walked back and forth over his body, stealing $60,000 worth of merchandise.

Finnegan immediately identified Sinclair from the composite picture.

Other police departments said they recognized the picture as a J.C. Weir (the alias Sinclair used), and Washington State listed a silver Pontiac registered to someone with that name. It had been surrendered in Wyoming, so Billings detectives contacted Wyoming officials, and there they found the silver Pontiac at the local airport. Inside was a .22-caliber handgun with a silencer and coin wrappings from Sparboe's shop.

In Jefferson County, Washington, officials were working on the 1986 disappearance of Robert and Dagmar Linton of Stockton, California, who had disappeared while they were camping on the Olympic Peninsula. A man was seen using the Lintons' credit cards to buy several items, including an expensive clarinet.

Sinclair's teenage daughter played the clarinet, and they discovered that her school records had been transferred from Washington to Alaska.

That's where they found Sinclair.

Investigators recovered Lucky Williams's driver's license; military ID card (he had been awarded a medal for meritorious service during the Vietnam War); and the keys to his house, car and business in a storage locker rented by Sinclair in Sumas, Washington. They also found receipts, ledger books and business records from Golden Hills Coin Exchange.

Before he could be brought to justice in the Reuben "Lucky" Williams case or any other, Charles Thurman Sinclair, who had a history of high blood pressure and heart problems, suffered a fatal heart attack on October 30, 1990, while awaiting extradition to Montana.

1995: The Tragic Murder of Dorothy Stone

Dorothy Stone was seventy-six years old in 1995 and had lived in Fairfield for nearly fifty years. She retired from the Bank of America in 1978 after having worked at both the Suisun City and Fairfield branches in numerous capacities for thirty-one years.

She and her husband, Robert, had no children, and after he died in 1991, she lived alone at 700 Nevada Street in a quiet neighborhood. Stone's biggest fear, according to one of her neighbors, was someone breaking into her house and harming her.

That's exactly what happened.

On the night of March 23, 1995, a neighbor arrived home from a trip to Reno at around 1:30 a.m. and noticed that Stone's side gate was open. She knew right away that something was amiss because leaving the gate open was something that Stone absolutely would not do. The neighbor, erring on the side of caution, immediately called the police.

Two officers arrived and discovered Stone dead in her bedroom. Pathologists searched the house and collected evidence, and the Solano County Coroner's Office conducted an autopsy. They would not reveal exactly how Stone had been killed except to say that it was "unusual." Stone had also been sexually assaulted. Nothing appeared to have been taken from the home, and it was unclear whether the attack was random or she was an intentional target.

The following day, Fairfield police revealed that Stone had been bludgeoned to death. They had the murder weapon but would not reveal it to the press.

The brutal manner of Stone's death was a gut punch to those that knew and loved her. She was described as generous and kind.

In the months after the murder, police sent more than 120 fingerprints to the Department of Justice for comparison. Then in January 1996, a Fairfield police technician faxed the fingerprints of eighteen-year-old Mario Stanford to the Department of Justice, and they matched the prints on Stone's door and the murder weapon.

Stone had been bludgeoned to death with her own twelve-inch black plastic television. Stanford was arrested, and the murder trial began the following year after a series of delays that included Stanford's public defender declaring a conflict of interest and withdrawing from the case.

Stanford's new public defender was able to get approval from the judge to use questionnaires when choosing a jury because of the widespread local coverage of the case. But right before the trial was set to start in October 1997, he said that the pool of 181 jurors did not include Vallejo and Benicia residents, which would seem to underrepresent Black people, whom he said made up approximately 16 percent of Solano County's population.

He argued that prosecutors had said that there may have been a racial motive for the murder. Dorothy Stone was white, and Mario Stanford was Black.

The Solano County Deputy district attorney believed the pool was fair and said Stanford's public defender had never explicitly raised the issue of race earlier. But the judge threw out the jury pool, and the process had to be repeated. The case finally went to trial in December.

The direct evidence of fingerprints on the murder weapon and in Stone's house was obviously damning, but what slammed the door shut on reasonable doubt was the testimony of a friend of Stanford's named Latroy Gates.

Gates had been interviewed earlier by Detective Rick Leonardini, who came armed with the sixty-six-page police report. In the interview, Gates said that Stanford had watched Dorothy Stone for years. He remembered Stanford talking about her when they attended Sullivan Middle School and watching her at her house and at local grocery stores.

"He was plotting on her and following her around," Gates was quoted as saying.

Gates told police that Stanford fixated on Stone because she resembled "some old white lady [that] had spit on his mother or grandmother in the past."

According to Gates, Stanford admitted to killing Stone, but Gates didn't believe it until he saw it in the newspaper. Gates said that Stanford told him that before delivering the fatal blows with the television, he had hit Stone with a jewelry box. That information had never been reported by local media.

Another item that was kept from the press was that a condom had been found under Stone's body, and Gates said he had seen Stanford with similar condoms.

Gates told the police that Stanford committed the heinous crimes and after leaving realized he'd forgotten his coat and went back inside to retrieve it. He saw that Stone was struggling to get up and realized she was not dead. That was when he bludgeoned her to death with the television set.

On the stand, Gates tried to recant his earlier testimony and assert that he made up lies to tell the police so they couldn't charge him as an accessory after the fact. He said that he could not recall saying things even when shown the police report. Because of his inconsistencies, the judge impeached Gates, which is a process whereby the court makes a formal finding that a witness contradicted themselves.

The trial lasted two weeks, and on December 22, 1997, after two days of deliberation, the jury declared Mario Stanford guilty of first-degree murder, sexual assault and burglary. The satisfaction with the verdict felt by Dorothy Stone's family and friends was short-lived, as in May 1998, a judge ruled that the jury committed misconduct by using a dictionary in their deliberations and granted Stanford's request for a new trial. An appellate court decided in September of that year that a new trial was not needed.

On November 21, 2024, Mario Stanford had a hearing at Pelican Bay State Prison and was granted parole.

1997: REVENGE MUTILATION

The case of John and Lorena Bobbitt captured international headlines in 1993. Lorena Bobbitt claimed that her husband had raped her and so she grabbed a Ginsu knife and sliced off his penis. It was later surgically reattached. A similar case, which drew the eyes of the world to Solano County's seat, happened four years later.

To set the stage for the Fairfield mutilation, it is necessary to go back to 1983. Albert Hall met a Suisun City woman named Denise Denofrio at a Suisun City bar. They went to the parking lot of Denny's on Holiday Lane to have sex in Denofrio's Chevelle, but Hall was unable to maintain an erection. When Denofrio teased him about his impotency, Hall strangled her to death with the cord from her sweatshirt.

Hall was identified as the suspect and later confessed to police. That confession was deemed inadmissible by a court for improper police procedure, and Hall pleaded guilty to voluntary manslaughter. He served half of a six-year prison sentence.

Fast-forward to December 4, 1997. According to Hall, he ran into an acquaintance named Brenda at a downtown Fairfield gas station. She agreed to go with him to his trailer, which was parked outside his brother's house. At about three o'clock on Friday morning, after they'd had sex, Brenda grabbed an X-ACTO knife and said that she had been friends with Denise Denofrio. In retaliation for Denise's murder, Brenda sliced off Hall's penis.

For hours, Hall tried to stop the bleeding before stumbling out onto the front lawn. A passerby spotted him eight hours after the attack. He was rushed to NorthBay Medical Center, but surgeons were not able to reattach the organ because it had been cut too close to the base.

Once Hall was medically stabilized, police questioned him. One central query was why a six-foot-tall, 180-pound man could not fight off a five-foot, seven-inch woman who weighed 135 pounds, per Hall's description of Brenda.

Killer cut own penis

Confesses to police he mutilated self; mysterious female attacker was a lie

The disturbing headline for a disturbing incident. *Fairfield Civic Center Library microfilm.*

Meanwhile, the story was picked up by the Associated Press; it exploded, and reporters flooded into the city.

The revenge penis-slicing story was irresistible to media outlets, but law enforcement was skeptical.

It all fell apart in a couple of days. Hall agreed to further questioning from police using a voice stress detector and admitted he had mutilated himself. Problems with alcohol, life stressors and obvious psychological issues all contributed to the sad incident.

It was revealed that Hall had been using methamphetamine the night of the incident.

Then retired Fairfield Police Detective John Mraz, who had investigated the Denofrio murder in 1983, was quoted in the *Daily Republic*: "I hope Mr. Hall gets the help he needs to find a reason for his continued existence. And I hope the Denofrio family can put this behind them and get on with their lives."

2011: THE SENSELESS MURDER OF HO KIM AT THE TRAVIS DAIRY

Fairfield's Holland Dairy Drive-In, located at 140 East Travis Boulevard, opened in 1959 and was an immediate local hit. It was a unique store but, unlike its name, wasn't a fast-food drive-in like Foster's Old-Fashion Freeze or A&W. In fact, it was a drive-thru that sold no fast food at all but "slow food" staples such as eggs, milk and bread. It's open-air, drive-thru service made it an extremely convenient convenience store.

Holland Dairy was originally owned by the Van Diemen family. They processed raw milk on-site by pasteurizing and homogenizing it and made whipping cream, half-and-half, chocolate milk and other products. They brought milk in glass jars to locals via their home delivery service and sold milk to every school in the county.

Holland Dairy's bow tie–shaped sign topped with a windmill became an iconic Fairfield image, and old photos of it often elicit remembrances of happy times from locals.

The Van Diemens ran Holland Dairy for about twenty years, leased it to others and then sold it. After changing hands numerous times, it eventually became the Travis Dairy.

Above: A painting of the old Holland Dairy Drive-In by painter and 1967 Armijo High grad Donna Covey. *Donna Covey Paintings*.

Opposite: A 2025 photo of the Travis Dairy, which has been shut down since 2011, when owner Ho Kim was killed. *Tony Wade*.

In 2011, the nostalgic memories of the old Holland Dairy were tainted by an atrocious crime. The owner of Travis Dairy at that time was seventy-year-old Ho J. Kim. Kim was affectionately called Papa by locals who frequented his establishment. He could often be seen reading his Bible in his store. On June 28, 2011, at about 7:50 p.m., Kim called 911 saying he had just been robbed and attacked. The assailants had pepper sprayed Kim and knocked him to the ground, where he hit his head. His attackers stole the cash register, a video recorder, cigarettes and several other items from the store.

Police responded quickly and saw Kim slumped over but could not enter the market immediately due to the heavy fog of pepper spray that hung inside. Although Kim was conscious when paramedics got to him, he soon became disoriented and later died of a heart attack. An autopsy showed it was likely due to the stress of the assault.

Five suspects, ranging in age from fifteen to eighteen, were arrested shortly after the incident. They were Dezmon Frazier, Osis Smith, James P. Young, James E. Williamson and Chelsea Johnson.

Frazier, Smith and Young had entered the store, assaulted Kim and stole merchandise and the cash register. Williamson was the lookout, and Johnson drove the getaway car. The crimes shocked and outraged locals, who placed cards and mementos at the store in honor of Kim. Fairfield newspaper coverage helped inadvertently fan the flames of anger when they repeatedly and inexplicably included the suspects' street names in reports of the incident, which many saw as hype.

James P. Young took a plea deal in 2012 where he pleaded no contest to charges of second-degree robbery, elder abuse carrying a vulnerable enhancement, conspiracy, false imprisonment and two counts of assault with a deadly weapon. He was sentenced to eighteen years and eight months in prison.

Frazier was sentenced to twenty-three years and eight months in prison after pleading no contest to the same charges as Young except he had three counts of assault with a deadly weapon. Johnson was given three years' probation after pleading no contest to involuntary manslaughter and second-degree robbery charges. Smith was sentenced to credit for his time already served. James E. Williamson, twenty-one, whose charges were eventually reduced to involuntary manslaughter and second-degree burglary, was sentenced to three years in county jail.

Several of the Travis Dairy defendants committed additional crimes after the incident that caused Ho Kim's death.

2013: Horror at Allan Witt Park

The shocking and appalling murder case of thirteen-year-old Genelle Conway-Allen is, in a way, the story of a contrast between two barbers: The first, a beloved local barber and civil servant who poured so much of his time and energy into helping Fairfield youth that the city's then biggest park was renamed after him. The second was a sadistic murderer who worked as a Fairfield barber, brutalized a child and callously dumped her nude body in the first barber's namesake park.

West Texas Street Park, a four-acre recreational space for locals that included a pool, called the Fairfield Plunge, opened on Memorial Day weekend in 1958. For decades, it was the go-to spot for sporting events, family barbecues and community events like the annual Fourth of July celebration or local Battle of the Bands competitions.

In 1973, West Texas Street Park was renamed Allan Witt Park in honor of the longtime Fairfield barber and city councilman Allan Witt, who was a stalwart advocate for youth. On February 1, 2013, the memories that longtime Fairfielders have of time with family, team members or friends at Allan Witt Park were tarnished by a grisly discovery.

A homeless man found the body of thirteen-year-old Genelle Renee Conway-Allen near the bathrooms on the Woolner Avenue side of the park and flagged down passing police officers. She had gone missing the previous day.

An autopsy revealed that she had been raped, sodomized and strangled to death before she was stripped and her nude body was dumped at the park.

Thirteen-year-old Genelle Conway-Allen, who was murdered in 2013. *Public domain.*

Genelle Conway-Allen had a rough life that was extinguished far too soon. She was in foster care because her biological parents struggled with addictions. What helped crack the case were electronic eyewitnesses to the abduction, the high-definition surveillance cameras along Fairfield's streets that were once considered quite controversial.

Genelle attended Green Valley Middle School and daily walked home along the same route. On the day of her disappearance, cameras recorded her walking home with a boy from school whom Fairfield police were able to identify and question. The boy told police that a car that pulled up next to them and the driver demanded that Genelle get inside. She began trembling and got into the car before the kidnapper sped away.

The boy's testimony matched up with the video footage, which also showed that the car had been following them for some time. Evidently, the kidnapper was waiting until there were no other witnesses. He hadn't counted on the cameras.

The suspect was identified as thirty-three-year-old Anthony Lemar Jones, a barber at Crowns Barber Shop in Fairfield. Police immediately put him under twenty-four-hour surveillance. With the eyes of law enforcement trained on him, Jones twice approached groups of young children walking home from school. He called out to them, but they did not respond.

Jones was arrested on February 8, 2013, and when questioned by police, he said he did not know the victim and never had sex with her. One of the detectives then showed Jones a photo of Genelle, and he recoiled from the picture and cried for almost an hour.

Jones's propensity for violence was highlighted by the fact that his wife, who was separated from him at the time of the murder, had filed a domestic violence restraining order against him three days before Genelle went missing. According to reports, she was so afraid of him that she once jumped out of a moving car to get away from him.

Allan Witt Park. *Tony Wade.*

A week after Genelle's murder, a crowd of locals held a vigil near the spot where her body was found. The approximately two hundred locals in attendance held candles and shared a moment of silence, and community leaders offered prayers.

DNA evidence was matched to Jones, and the District Attorney's Office discussed making it a death penalty case. Legal wrangling resulted in the case slowly working its way through the system for years. In May 2016, Jones pleaded guilty to a murder charge in exchange for a punishment of life in prison without the possibility of parole to avoid the death penalty.

At his sentencing, members of Jones's family were allowed to speak, although they were informed by the judge that whatever they had to say would have no effect on the punishment that would be meted out. Jones's brother repeatedly called his sibling "my hero." The judge bristled at that and, when handing down the sentence, said, "Mr. Jones is nobody's hero."

One of Genelle's aunts said, "I hope he spends every day of the rest of his life feeling torture and pain and loneliness and emptiness." Anthony Lemar Jones, BA3875, has been incarcerated at the California State Prison at Corcoran since July 2016.

6
FAIRFIELD CITY COUNCIL CRIMES

A series of criminal activity that involved Fairfield City Council members (and one candidate) was a rough stretch in the long history of municipal public service in Solano County's seat. From 1999 to 2008, the events ranged from public drunkenness to felony drug possession, fraud and assault. Ultimately this chapter is about the human failings that all of us, including elected officials, have and the resilience of the Fairfield community. It's important to point out that while the shocking and senseless murder of Fairfield City Councilman Matt Garcia is included here, he was obviously a victim, not a perpetrator.

George Pettygrove—A Series of Unfortunate Incidents

In 2010, when former Fairfield Mayor George Pettygrove passed away at the age of seventy-nine, he was remembered as a straight shooter who loved the city he served and lived in for more than fifty years. Pettygrove, a U.S. Navy veteran of the Korean War, worked as a Fairfield educator for over three decades.

Petty was appointed to finish out the Fairfield City Council term of his wife, Joy, who died in office in 1991. He was elected mayor in 1997.

In 1999, the city council and city officials were engaged in contentious monthslong negotiations over contracts and pay raises for police officers.

The Harry T. Price Memorial Council Chamber. *Tony Wade.*

It was in that tense environment when a series of unfortunate incidents occurred.

On September 13, 1999, Pettygrove, then sixty-five years old, had a few drinks at a Fairfield Chamber of Commerce mixer and left around 7:00 or 8:00 p.m. While driving home at 2:00 a.m., he stopped about two blocks from his house to avoid driving past California Highway Patrol officers investigating a driver (ironically) for a DUI. They noticed Pettygrove standing outside his vehicle and noted that he appeared unsteady and intoxicated.

Pettygrove identified himself as the mayor of Fairfield, and the officers drove him home. When they arrived, Pettygrove told them he didn't have his keys and had left his garage door opener in his truck. The officers left him on his front porch to get the garage door opener from his vehicle, and when they returned, Pettygrove was bleeding from a cut on his head. He had apparently tripped and hit his head on a brick planter in front of his house.

He was then airlifted by helicopter to the UC Davis Medical Center. This all created a spectacle for Pettygrove's neighbors.

Per procedure, the Fairfield police planned to issue a press release the next day about the mayor's accident. A draft described Pettygrove as "uncooperative" and "combative" and said that the doctor who treated him at the hospital called him "inebriated." City officials vetoed the FPD's statement and issued their own, which excluded the fact that Pettygrove had been drinking.

The Fairfield Police Officers' Association promptly called for the mayor's resignation and took the city manager and others to task for withholding how Pettygrove's intoxicated state played into the whole series of events. The city fired back that the union was just playing politics with the situation because of the contract negotiations.

An editorial in the *Daily Republic* took the city to task for how they handled the whole situation:

> *City administrators should be ashamed. Embarrassing incidents happen to anyone, including public officials. Should the mayor have been drinking and driving, if that's what happened? No. And he knows it.*
>
> *But equally damning is the city's efforts to cover up the incident. Acknowledge the problem, be honest about the facts, and get on with it. Don't treat citizens like children who can't be trusted with the truth.*

That Friday, September 17, 1999, in a one-page note Mayor Pettygrove apologized to the residents of Fairfield for the embarrassment he caused the city. He thanked police and emergency workers for coming to his aid, adding that he asked for no special treatment because of his office. Pettygrove acknowledged that he had serious issues that he needed deal with. He added that he had no intention of resigning.

While the public apology took a little of the sting out of the events, controversy remained. Many wondered why he was not charged with drunk driving or public intoxication at the least. Other council members like Karin MacMillan reported getting calls from Fairfielders who didn't buy that Pettygrove hadn't asked for special treatment. "One person who called had a DUI and had to pay lots of money. He didn't get a free ride home."

Pettygrove remained the Fairfield mayor until 2001, when he was defeated by MacMillan.

JOHN ENGLISH—THE PRICE OF ADDICTION

There are good ways and bad ways to ring in the new year. Surely one of the worst ways is to be arrested for drug possession at the airport. That is what happened to then Fairfield City Councilman John English on December 31, 2004. The narcotics and paraphernalia were found inside a shoe in English's carry-on bag as he was planning to take a red-eye Jet Blue flight to New York City. He was on the way to celebrate the promotion of a cousin to the rank of brigadier general in the air force. Airport security spotted the suspicious substance, which turned out to be 4.8 grams of crystal meth and two drug pipes.

John English was a successful businessman who grew his company, Auto Logistics Solutions Inc., from a startup to a multimillion-dollar entity. English was elected to the city council in 2001 and was a popular city councilman who was dedicated to his constituents, to the community's youth and to protecting the victims of domestic violence. He was heavily involved in advocating for a Boys & Girls Club of America and for more police for the city.

After his arrest, English's fellow council members Jack Batson, Mayor Karin MacMillan and Harry Price all expressed their shock. After he posted his $3,000 bail, English did a television interview in which he said the drugs were not his and implicated his thirty-year-old nephew, who lived with him in his Rancho Solano home.

English said that when he suspected his nephew was using drugs, he confronted the young man, who confessed and agreed to get help. He allegedly told English he had destroyed the drugs and tossed the paraphernalia into a nearby pond. English contended that what really happened was that his

Drugs not mine, says Fairfield official

Meth found at airport belonged to nephew, councilman argues; arraignment's set for Friday.

John English

"It's ugly and embarrassing," the Fairfield City Council member said of his arrest at Sacramento's airport Friday.

Fairfield City Councilman John English declares that drugs found in his belongings at the airport were not his. *Fairfield Civic Center Library microfilm.*

nephew inexplicably hid the drugs in English's bedroom among his personal possessions. His nephew backed up English's explanation to authorities.

At the next city council meeting, there were local and regional newspeople everywhere. English apologized for the circus-like atmosphere and said he would fight the charges and be exonerated.

At his trial, English acted as his own attorney. Airport security screeners testified they had started to do a partial search of English's belongings after the X-ray screening but decided to perform a full search after English started to sweat, was verbally abusive and wanted to leave the airport. He was quoted as saying, "While you are distracting me you could have planted something in my bag."

The prosecution took the unusual step of testing the drug pipes for DNA. What they found matched English. His explanation was that his spittle must have gotten on them during an animated "come to Jesus" talk with his nephew.

Most damaging to English was the fact that his nephew, who at first said the drugs and pipes were his, recanted and testified against his uncle. English attempted to discredit his nephew during the trial by showing he had a drug problem.

In July 2005, English was convicted in Sacramento Superior Court of possession of methamphetamine and drug paraphernalia and for inducing his nephew to take the fall for him. He resigned from the city council.

In a bid to overturn the conviction and get a new trial, English floated the bizarre theory that his nephew had lied to the jury because he thought he was part of a reality show. He said that his nephew thought that by testifying falsely he would win $1 million.

At his sentencing on August 17, 2005, Judge James L. Long sentenced English to thirty days in jail and three years' probation. The judge gave the nod to the mitigating circumstance of English's years of hard work and public service. The deputy district attorney had requested 180 days in jail because English continued to insist he did nothing wrong, showed no remorse and tried to manipulate the justice system by sacrificing a member of his own family.

The judge said English could do a work furlough program where he continued to do his job and do his jail time at nights and on the weekends. He could have reduced the felony to a misdemeanor but decided against it.

English dabbed at his eyes as tears fell.

"I'll give you the ability to reduce it, depending on your conduct—I hope you don't make me look silly," the judge said.

Those turned out to be prophetic words.

On August 29, 2005, English was arrested at Cache Creek Casino. He had reported losing his travel bag there. A casino employee came across it near a slot machine and turned it into security. Inside there were three grams of methamphetamine. When English was first asked if the bag was his, he said it was. After they told him he had to come with them, he started to deny it. Unfortunately for English, everything at the casino was videorecorded and security confirmed the bag was his.

Fairfield City Councilman John English dabbing tears at his sentencing in 2005. *Fairfield Civic Center Library microfilm.*

English was arrested on suspicion of possessing a controlled substance, posted $10,000 bail and was released from the Yolo County jail but was subsequently brought back in for violation of his probation. When he appeared in front of the judge on the new charges, his orange jumpsuit was a stark contrast to the stylish three-piece suits he had worn at his first trial. In a probation report, English finally admitted to using methamphetamine since the summer of 2003. He had started using it once every two to three weeks before it became a daily habit.

English was sentenced to six months. He said at his sentencing, "My misuse of the system was a grave error in judgment guided by drug use, not malice."

After doing his time, English moved to Southern California and in 2006 had a phone conversation with longtime *Daily Republic* opinion columnist (and the author's brother) Kelvin Wade. Parts of that call were subsequently printed in Wade's column "The Other Side." English said it was arrogance that led him to thinking he could handle his addiction. He had been approached before his arrests with offers of help, but had brushed them off. The former city councilman offered a message for the people of Fairfield: "I would simply like to say that I apologize for lying and betraying the public's trust. My apology is offered without qualification or excuses."

English cleaned up and kept his company going. In 2007, he became a regional vice president of the American Arbitration Association, a position he held until retiring eleven years later.

PAUL RANDHAWA—RUNNING FOR CITY COUNCIL FROM A JAIL CELL

One does not have to be a political pro to know that a good rule of thumb as a candidate is not to get arrested the day before an election. Evidently, Fairfield City Council candidate Igbal Paul Randhawa never got that memo.

On November 7, 2005, Randhawa, who was running for one of the two open seats on the Fairfield City Council, was arrested with his wife and son by San Francisco law enforcement officials. Randhawa, fifty-two, was booked into Solano County Jail on suspicion of fifteen counts of grand theft, fifteen counts of failing to refund money and one count of conspiracy. His bail was set at $1 million.

Gurdev "Debbie" K. Randhawa, forty-four, and Manjinder "Manny" Randhawa, twenty-two, both were booked on suspicion of eleven counts

Council candidate arrested

Paul Randhawa held on $1 million bail for alleged fraud

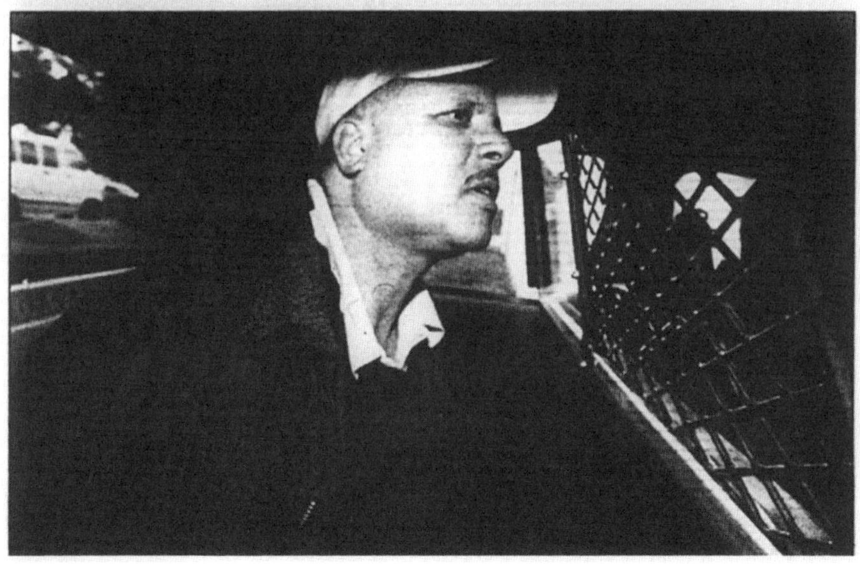

Fairfield city council candidate Paul Randhawa being arrested the day before the 2005 election in which he was running. *Fairfield Civic Center Library microfilm.*

of grand theft, eleven counts of failing to refund money and one count of conspiracy. Their bail was $500,000 each.

The family, co-owners of Fairfield-based M&K Travel Services Inc., were accused of bilking at least fifteen people out of a total of more than $50,000 between May 2004 and June 2005. Victims reportedly never received their tickets and, in two instances, apparently received refund checks that bounced.

The company, which advertised discount travel to India, had been under investigation since 2004. The state attorney general's office reportedly worked with Fairfield police before sending the case to San Francisco County District Attorney Kamala Harris in June 2005.

In a jailhouse interview, Randhawa proclaimed his innocence and claimed the arrest was "definitely politically motivated."

"Candidates, more than one, have done this to me," he said, refusing to name who he suspected.

Randhawa also complained that the bail amount was excessive. Officials responded that the bail was set based on the amount of money stolen and subsequent risk for flight because of his connection to India.

Prosecutors said that Randhawa's travel agency schemed to discourage customers from paying for tickets with credit cards by quoting lower prices if cash or cashier's checks were used instead. M&K Travel then issued customers an email itinerary with a confirmation number, but when customers called the airline to confirm their flight, they were told there were no tickets in their name. Customers asking Randhawa's business for a refund got the runaround.

While officials searched the company's West Texas Street office for evidence, an M&K Travel customer walked into the office and told a familiar story. He said his mother had ordered two plane tickets to Boston through the agency a week before. When she called the airline to buy a third seat, she found that the airline had no record of her other ticket purchases. Investigators gave the man their phone number and wished him luck on getting his mother's money back.

Meanwhile, court documents indicated the Randhawas had a history of legal battles—mostly civil matters—dating back to 1993. At least two of eleven lawsuits alleged the travel agency owed thousands of dollars to creditors.

Iqbal Randhawa eventually pleaded guilty to grand theft and forgery charges and was sentenced to three years in state prison. His wife pleaded guilty to one count of grand theft and was sentenced to thirty days in San Francisco County Jail. Manjinder Randhawa also pleaded guilty to one count of grand theft and was sentenced to 480 hours of community service.

The family was also ordered to pay $114,000 in restitution to the victims of the 2004–05 scam.

Two years later, they were arrested again on similar charges.

As for the 2005 Fairfield City Council election, Paul Randhawa came in last place with 1,714 votes.

MATT GARCIA—KEEP THE DREAM ALIVE

What lifelong Fairfield resident Matt Garcia was able to accomplish in 2007—winning a seat on the Fairfield City Council—was nothing short of incredible. When he kicked off his campaign, he was a twenty-year-old bank employee with no political experience—unless you counted being vice-president of his senior class at Armijo High School in 2004. It was easy to write him off if you practiced contempt prior to investigation, as some locals did.

But Fairfielders who had been in Matt Garcia's presence were immediately struck if not smitten by his charisma and impressed by his drive to better the city that he loved. Garcia was able to build a credible campaign machine that featured a coalition of youth, seniors and those between who bought into his vision, his dream, for Fairfield. Garcia's plans included cleaning up the city, focusing on creating youth activities to steer them away from crime and gangs and improving the quality of life for all residents.

Matt Garcia's city council portrait. *The Matt Garcia Foundation.*

Fairfield Mayor Harry Price said in 2007, "Matt is one of those who can walk into any setting, whether a group of young people in a park or a senior center and just light up the room. He was blessed with an incredible smile, a sharp intellect and the ability to relate to all ages and ethnic groups."

While Garcia no doubt appreciated the mayor's endorsement, he also had his eye on Price's job. In fact, he had prophesied that he would become the mayor of Fairfield—when he was in sixth grade.

Despite being heavily outspent in the election, Matt Garcia defeated a two-term incumbent businessman and, at twenty-one, became the youngest person ever elected to the Fairfield City Council. His goal of one day becoming Mayor Garcia was no longer a pipe dream but an attainable goal.

But tragically it was not to be.

On the night of September 1, 2008, Matt was visiting a female friend in the Cordelia Villages section of Fairfield when he was shot in the head in a case of mistaken identity. Fairfielders who had been captivated by the infectious optimism that Garcia's candidacy and victory represented were stunned and devastated.

SPORTS: NADAL TAKEN TO FOUR SETS AT U.S. OPEN, B1 · UCLA DOWNS NO. 18 TENNESSEE IN OVERTIME, B2

TUESDAY, SEPTEMBER 2, 2008 FAIRFIELD-SUISUN 50 CENTS

DAILY REPUBLIC

WWW.DAILYREPUBLIC.COM

Councilman Garcia shot

22-year-old in critical condition after drive-by

By Ben Antonius and Audrey Wong
Daily Republic

FAIRFIELD — Fairfield City Councilman Matt Garcia was shot in the head and critically wounded in a drive-by shooting late Monday night in Cordelia Villages.

GARCIA

Firefighters were able to get Garcia's vital signs at the scene. Garcia, 22, was transported by helicopter to John Muir Medical Center in Walnut Creek in critical condition. He was in the intensive care unit as of press time.

"I am absolutely numb," said Councilman Chuck Timm, a retired police sergeant who was elected the same day as Garcia. "He is so young and he is so good for this city, especially with the youth. He could relate to the 13-year-old African-American or Hispanic girl or boy and a 54-year-old fat, white guy like me. He just has that ability to draw people together."

The shooting occurred at 8:30 p.m. Witnesses said Garcia was visiting a female friend on the 5000 block of Silverado Drive and was getting out of his car when someone in a passing car fired several shots, police officials said. The female friend called 911.

City officials said Garcia's family members had been notified and were at the hospital. Mayor Harry Price, City Manager Sean Quinn and Fire Chief Vince Webster also drove to Walnut Creek following the shooting.

In a hastily arranged press conference at nearby Rodriguez High School, police said they had no motive for the shooting and did not know whether Garcia was the intended target.

"We will catch you, we will hunt you down, we will spare no resources," Police Chief Kenton Rainey said.

Police closed a large portion of Silverado Drive immediately following the shooting. Officials did not offer information on the nature of Garcia's relationship with the female friend, nor the weapon

See Garcia, Back Page

Chris Jordan/Daily Republic

Police examine the crime scene where Fairfield City Councilman Matt Garcia was shot Monday night on the 5000 block of Silverado Drive.

The front page of the September 2, 2008 *Daily Republic. Fairfield Civic Center Library microfilm.*

Garcia had beaten the odds when it came to being elected, but the odds of coming back from a head shot were too great. He was declared brain dead, and his family made the difficult decision to remove him from life support. His organs were donated so that even in death he gave hope to others.

The refreshing wave of local optimism that Garcia's election ushered in made his senseless murder even more crushing. His funeral was held on Brownlee Field at Armijo High School, and so many attended there was an overflow area set up in the school's gymnasium. A Police Activities League (PAL) youth center that was almost ready to open was renamed from the Billy G. Yarbrough Youth Center to the Matt Garcia Teen Center at the

THE OTHER SIDE

Garcia was lightning in a bottle

Kelvin Wade

The death of Councilman Matt Garcia is a nightmare for his family, his friends and the community. How could we be saying goodbye to one of our most enthusiastic, warm, dynamic young leaders?

I've always tried to give readers more light than heat in this column but I can't make any promises in light of the killing of Matt Garcia. I'm angry.

I'm desk-trashing, wall-punching, profanity-spewing angry that an inspirational young leader was cut down by some cowardly punk. A worthless human being has taken the life of a priceless one. I've found myself hoping that police find the perpetrator armed and have to take him out. If the attack was gang-related, I've caught myself deriving satisfaction out of street justice being done to the assailant. What Fairfield jury would convict someone who punished Matt's killer?

But taking a step back, I know that an eye for an eye leaves everyone blind. I know that to hope for street justice just increases the violence on our streets and raises the possibility of more innocents being caught in the crossfire. I know that it only perpetuates an endless cycle of violence. I know that hate in my heart only harms me, not the person who did this.

And I also know what Matt Garcia stood for.

When I first met Matt last year, expecting to find some narcissistic kid playing City Council candidate, boy, was I mistaken. Over sandwiches at Joe's Buffet, I was convinced that not only was I sitting with the next Fairfield City Council member, but I was sitting with a future Mayor, Congressman, the sky was the limit.

A month or so ago, after having lunch with Councilmen John Mraz and Matt Garcia, my brother Tony and I hung around outside the Blue Frog talking about Garcia. We were both so impressed with his energy, his focus and his skill set. Garcia was lightning in a bottle. You could tell he was going places.

Matt's smile was infectious. He had a way of making you feel like you were his closest friend. And he used that charm to bring people together.

It's a tragedy when any innocent person is the victim of a violent crime. However, in Matt's case the pain is made that much more acute because he had dedicated his life to fighting the very thing that took his. He wanted to build a safe Fairfield for everyone and wanted to raise his own children here.

While this horror has galvanized us, we must act. Fairfield has to crackdown on violence. If that means opening our wallets for more cops, organizing citizen patrols, and participating in Neighborhood Watch, residents must partner with the police to fight crime.

The community has lost so much potential this week. Just last week, Matt wrote the following on his Myspace page: "I have been thinking about my life and it is not complete, but it is getting there. I thought about the things I have accomplished over the years; it has truly been a blessing. It just shows people when you put your mind to something you can make it happen. I still haven't accomplished everything, but I am working toward it and I believe if it is God's will, it will happen."

It hurts so deeply and feels like hope itself has died. But as my brother Tony told me on Tuesday, "Matt has inspired too many people to let hope die. But hope took a beating today."

It's up to us to continue Matt's work. Peace.

Kelvin Wade is a writer and lives in Fairfield. Visit his blog at www.dailyrepublic.typepad.com/theotherside or e-mail him at kelvinjwade@aol.com

Daily Republic columnist Kelvin Wade's column on Matt Garcia in 2008. *Fairfield Civic Center Library microfilm.*

insistence of the Yarbrough family. There was a determination to not let Matt's dream die with him. That was the catalyst for his mother, Teresa Taylor Courtemanche, and stepfather Raymond Courtemanche to form the Matt Garcia Foundation.

But there was also the business of justice.

Within three weeks, the trio responsible for the horrible crime were captured. Henry Don Williams, thirty-two; his pregnant girlfriend Nicole Stewart, thirty-three; and Gene Allen Combs, forty-five, were arrested for the murder.

Stewart was the driver of the vehicle they were in when the murder took place. At trial Stewart said that she and Williams had met Combs at a Fairfield fast-food restaurant on the day of the killing. He had complained that a drug dealer she identified as Ryan Estes had cheated him out of fifty dollars.

The trio then drove to the alleged dealer's house on Silverado Drive in the Cordelia area, but he wasn't there. They were about to leave when a Cadillac pulled up about fifty yards away and a man got out. Combs told Williams that the man wasn't Estes, but Williams exited the vehicle where Garcia stood in a driveway and fired numerous rounds before getting back in the sedan and speeding off.

Williams was an ex-convict who served prison time in California for violently resisting a law enforcement officer and had done time in Nevada for forgery. He was on probation for a misdemeanor drunken-driving conviction in Fairfield at the time he murdered Garcia.

Jurors in Williams's two-week trial deliberated for several days before returning their verdict in the Vallejo courtroom of Judge Robert Bowers. In addition to the murder charge, Williams was found guilty of the enhancement of using a gun. He was sentenced to a term of fifty years to life in prison. The judge also fined Williams $10,000 and ordered him to pay $20,000 in restitution to the City of Fairfield, the Garcia family and the state Victims Compensation Board.

Teresa Courtemanche and her son Matt Garcia. *The Matt Garcia Foundation.*

Combs was later found guilty of second-degree murder for aiding and abetting the killing and was

Teresa Courtemanche at a Matt Garcia Foundation gun buyback event. *The Matt Garcia Foundation.*

sentenced to fifteen years to life. Nicole Stewart took a controversial plea deal whereby she agreed to testify against her co-defendants and was never charged with any crime. After her testimony, she was placed in a witness protection program.

The murder of Matt Garcia victimized his family, friends and constituency and kept spreading in a ripple effect, as it did not end after those responsible were brought to justice. Williams has been a particular thorn in the side of the immediate family, as he has sought countless appeals that have been shot down as meritless but retraumatize those who loved Matt. In addition to the legal actions, Williams changed his name, wrote a book about himself and showed no remorse.

On the other end of the spectrum is Gene Combs, who turned himself in twelve days after the murder and sought to better himself while in prison. To be sure, the incentive to be freed from incarceration is a carrot for such behavior, but few inmates actually pursue self-improvement. In 2016, the Courtemanches met with him in prison, and he was released in 2020.

The Matt Garcia Foundation was created to "support youth, stop crime and strengthen the community." These are the principles on which Garcia based his campaign and lived his life. The foundation's numerous activities and programs have included the Matt Garcia Career and College Academy, an annual fundraising golf tournament, a monthly downtown cleanup, scholarships for high school seniors and a gun buyback program. Several current members of the foundation who give hands and feet to his dream are too young to ever have known Matt.

At Henry Don Williams's sentencing, Teresa Courtemanche told him directly, "You did not kill his spirit; you are not capable of doing that." The ongoing community-building work of the Matt Garcia Foundation continues to keep the fallen councilman's dream alive.

Frank Kardos—Losing It All

September 2008 was a particularly rough month for the residents of Fairfield. It started out with the tragic murder of Matt Garcia, but another city councilmember died that month.

Fairfield City Councilman Frank Kardos was arrested on January 20, 2007, on a felony charge of assault with a deadly weapon and a misdemeanor charge of domestic violence involving a former girlfriend.

Kardos was a vice-principal at Armijo High School at that time and was placed on paid administrative leave. After the arrest involving his former girlfriend, details of alleged abuse involving Kardos's ex-wife emerged. They included choking, spitting and other physical and mental abuse during the thirteen-year marriage.

While their divorce was being finalized, his ex-wife sought a restraining order and Kardos attended anger management classes.

At his trial, Kardos's ex-girlfriend began crying as soon as she was asked to point him out in the courtroom. She described the couple's on-again-off-again relationship that ended on January 19, 2007, when he grabbed her by the neck, slammed her head against the headboard of her bed and then choked her until she nearly lost consciousness. After the attack, she got a burglar alarm, built a fence around her house, carried pepper spray and even moved out of her home for several weeks.

Kardos's ex-wife testified that he regularly assaulted her before, during and after their thirteen-year marriage. She detailed several assault incidents that involved Kardos slamming her head against walls or furniture.

Kardos testified that his ex-girlfriend was the one who lost control and slapped him and kicked him in the groin. Kardos's two sons, aged twelve and fifteen, testified on his behalf.

Kardos and the victim agreed on three things about the incident in question: Kardos had come to her home to be consoled about the death of his uncle, they made love and then they fell asleep.

The ex-girlfriend went to a Vallejo hospital the following day and was treated for a concussion but did not contact police about the assault because of a concern that it might harm Kardos's political ambitions. Hospital staff contacted Fairfield police.

Kardos had been arrested in 2003 and charged with domestic battery, but the case was dismissed the following week. He had also been arrested in 1999 on suspicion of domestic battery. The district attorney's office did not prosecute due to insufficient evidence.

It took the jury about two hours to reach the verdict after a four-day trial. Kardos was found guilty of felony assault and misdemeanor battery.

As the verdict was read, Kardos gave a heavy sigh, his jaw dropped open and his head sunk to his chest. He was acutely aware that a felony conviction would cost him his teaching credential and his seat on the

Conviction to cost councilman

Brad Zweerink Daily Republic

Fairfield Councilman Frank Kardos, right, sits with his attorney Daniel Russo in Solano County Court after a jury found him guilty of felony assault and misdemeanor battery Friday afternoon. Russo plans to appeal the ruling.

Daily Republic article when Fairfield City Councilman Frank Kardos was found guilty of felony assault and misdemeanor battery. Kardos died by suicide the next day. *Fairfield Civic Center Library microfilm.*

Fairfield City Council. On top of that, he was facing a potential four-year prison sentence.

The prosecutor in the case criticized Kardos for dragging his two sons into the case as defense witnesses. He told the jury that the boys' testimony was obviously rehearsed and implied that they had testified because they feared their father's wrath.

After the verdict was read, prosecutors asked that Kardos be immediately remanded into custody, but the judge denied their request.

The next day, Frank Kardos hanged himself. His body was found by one of his sons.

The District Attorney's Office said after Kardos's body was found that their denied remand request was not meant to be punitive but was intended to protect his former wife, his former girlfriend, his children and himself. They recognized that the verdict meant he would lose his job and his political career and there was a strong likelihood for catastrophic behavior.

7
LAWMEN LOOK BACK ON TRUE CRIMES

I fought the law, and the law won.
—The Crickets

The earliest known police force was created in Egypt around 3000 BCE. The pharaoh appointed an official for security and justice to each of the empire's forty-two administrative jurisdictions. The official was assisted by a chief of police, known as the *sab heri seker*, or "chief of the hitters."

The Solano County Sheriff's Office was born in 1850 when Solano County became one of California's original twenty-seven counties at the time of statehood. In the first election on April 1, 1850, Sheriff Francis Drake Brown won with 88 out of 176 votes. A sheriff's mounted posse was started in 1947 and still exists to this day. The crimes handled by the men and women of the Solano County Sheriff's department over their long history run the gamut from hog theft to hit-and-runs to homicide.

Stanley Emerson—Sheriff's Department Memories

Author's note: My jaw hit the floor when I learned from a friend that a Fairfield family, the Emersons, lived in the jail because that is what the Solano County undersheriff did. It turned out they were not the first to do so, but the fact that Stanley and Lillian Emerson had two young daughters made it an interesting story that needed to be told. I interviewed

Judy Emerson Gosselin, the oldest daughter, in 2013 and published "The Family That Lived in the Solano County Jail."

Years later I interviewed Judy's father, retired Solano County Undersheriff Stanley Emerson, when he was one hundred years old. Now, Stanley's hearing was shot, so for us to communicate, Judy had to repeat my questions very loudly or type them onto an electronic tablet. But his memory was amazingly pristine. Like former President Ronald Reagan, when it comes to interviews with people about long ago events, I practice the old Russian proverb: doveryai, no proveryai *(*доверяй, но проверяй*) meaning "trust, but verify." When I checked the primary sources, Stanley Emerson's accounts were almost completely accurate.*

Stanley Merle Emerson was born in Westwood, California, in Lassen County (which, fun fact, is the home of mythical lumberjack Paul Bunyan). The Red River Lumber Company built the entire town, including a skating rink, Masonic Hall and theater.

Ironically, as a young man, Emerson had a few run-ins with the law. Nothing serious, but he was a bit of a local scamp given to mischievous shenanigans. For example, when warned by the highway patrol to make his motorcycle street legal, he opted to outrun law enforcement through the town's alleys.

He later got a car, installed a piercingly loud whistle tip on the exhaust and hit it when passing by the highway patrolman's house at midnight. The mechanical acumen that manifested itself in Emerson's orneriness as a young man would later serve him well as a Solano County crime fighter.

Emerson moved to Vallejo and began building submarines at Mare Island Naval Shipyard. He finished a four-year apprenticeship as a shipfitter with a year to spare.

In 1939 he met his future wife, Lillian, at a dance held at the S.C.D.E.S. Portuguese Hall in Vallejo. They eloped in 1942 and stayed together sixty-one years until Lillian's death in 2003.

During World War II, Emerson joined the navy and served on the submarine USS *Mendhaven*. When the global conflict ended, he returned to his job at Mare Island. He was frustrated by being assigned to "bum jobs" instead of working on subs, so he made a career change.

"I had a buddy that was a police officer, and boy, I thought that uniform looked pretty slick. I decided to give it a shot. I was making a good salary as a shipfitter and had to start out with peanuts at the sheriff's department. I was originally assigned to Vallejo, and it was more to my liking when I moved to Fairfield."

The Solano County Sheriff's Posse in a parade on Texas Street in 1969. *History of the Solano County Sheriff's Office Facebook page.*

Back in those days, the sheriff's department owned a few cars, but deputies like Emerson had to drive their own vehicles. Emerson drove a Chevrolet with a "great big siren I think they took off an old fire truck."

"I worked a shift in the day and then if I got a call at night, I took the family car and went out by myself, no backup," Emerson said.

One time Emerson got a call from the highway patrol about some jail escapees in a Chrysler. On Highway 40 in Vacaville, Emerson used his Chevy and a fruit truck he'd commandeered to set a roadblock. The escapees lost control of the Chrysler and became wedged under the fruit truck as Emerson and a special deputy fired pistols at them.

Emerson used new techniques to solve cases, and an early example was the case of a man who'd stolen some cattle and changed their brand using acid. At trial, the man surprised everyone by producing what appeared to be a legitimate bill of sale.

"So I took it to the crime lab in Sacramento, and they used infrared photography and found the original writing, which had been erased and

Left, Solano County Undersheriff Stanley Emerson in younger days; *right*, with his daughters Susan and Judy. *Judy Emerson Gosselin.*

written over. I talked to a handwriting expert and had exemplars of this guy's wife and his sister. The expert testified that the sister had forged it. He pled guilty."

Around 1937, Fairfielders Onis James Lentz and his wife, Ida May, opened the Octo Inn, a restaurant and gas station, near what in 2025 is the corner of West Texas Street and Beck Avenue. It was called the Octo Inn because it was an eight-sided building.

While hamburgers and homemade pies were their specialties, the Octo Inn became known not for their food but for being a burglar magnet. That was probably due to its then relatively isolated location away from the heart of Fairfield and close to the getaway route of U.S. 40. A January 1954 newspaper article stated that the Octo Inn had been burglarized twenty times in nineteen years.

"It was the perfect spot to commit burglary, but we caught all of them. I even drilled a hole in the wall so if someone tried to hole up in the bathroom, I could shoot some tear gas in there. We put mirrors behind the bar so you could see if someone was crouched back there hiding, and that got a few. It got to the point where I would go to San Quentin with a prisoner, and they would say, 'Is this another Octo Inn deal?'"

Stanley Emerson became Solano County undersheriff in 1955, and his family moved from their home on Taylor Street in Fairfield to an upstairs apartment in the Solano County jail. His wife, Lillian, became the jail's matron and attended to female prisoners. Their daughters, Judy and Susan, were then both preteens, and the walls in their bedroom featured wallpaper with ballerinas in pink, blue and yellow tutus—a stark contrast to the other walls in the facility. The girls found living in the jail exciting, but their father's response was tempered.

"It wasn't all peaches and cream. The cell block was right next door, and the drunk tank was downstairs. When you got a really noisy drunk, it reverberated when they beat on the door," Emerson said.

Emerson helped solve numerous cases during his thirty-four years with the sheriff's office.

In 1967, the sheriff's office busted a ring of mercury thieves who were stealing the valuable mineral from PG&E natural gas wells in several different counties. On the Liberty Island well near Rio Vista, Emerson rigged a wire so it tripped an alert at the sheriff's office when someone tampered with it. One night, it went off, and various law enforcement agencies assembled with their lights off and at a deep depression in the road, where they confronted the thieves.

"I opened the trunk, and there was mercury in a container. They said they didn't know how it got there. I went to my car and got a black light. What they didn't know was I'd put fluorescent dye there [on the well] and it was all over them. They lit up like a Christmas tree."

A postcard of San Quentin State Prison. No one wrote "Wish you were here!" on the other side. *Public domain.*

Then there was the Great Grain Robbery. In northern Solano County, along the railroad tracks a Tremont warehouse reported repeated thefts.

"I noticed they came in the same door so I took a common mousetrap and soldered a lead to the door and the other I soldered to an army field phone. I ran the wire down the railroad tracks about three-quarters of a mile to a section house. I put a common doorbell in there and hooked it up to juice. I told a man who lived nearby if it rings to call the sheriff's office."

Former Solano County Undersheriff Stanley Emerson's uniform and pictures at his one hundredth birthday party. *Judy Emerson Gosselin.*

One night it rang, so the sheriffs gathered and lay in wait. When they suddenly turned on their lights, there was a truck loaded with 117 sacks of grain and one startled thief with a grain sack in his arms. Another man ran into the warehouse.

"The department had one machine gun, and a deputy pointed it up at the tin roof and let it rip, yelling, 'Come outta there you sonofabitch!'" Emerson said.

Emerson retired in 1980. A resolution signed by Assemblyman Thomas Hannigan praised him for establishing the department's first identification section and photo/crime lab, initializing the first indexed record-keeping system in the department, instituting the first formalized martial arts training program and originating and supervising a firearms training program in a rock quarry using hand-drawn targets.

He also founded the department's first Special Weapons and Tactics (SWAT) squad.

Emerson became a centenarian on April 26, 2019, and celebrated with three parties.

When asked if he ever thought he'd live to be one hundred years old, Emerson replied, "I figured I was gonna be pretty close. I didn't give up my motorcycle until I was ninety-three!"

Stanley Emerson died on November 15, 2023, at the age of 104.

FAIRFIELD POLICE DEPARTMENT

Fairfield became incorporated on December 7, 1903, and a month later the municipal authorities passed Ordinance No. 5, which spelled out the duties of the Fairfield town marshal. They included keeping the peace, being a process server, prosecuting crimes and collecting funds from various license taxes.

From 1931 to 1943, Fairfield had one police officer named Howard Yatsie (pronounced yight-see). It was Fairfield's closest approximation to Andy Taylor, sheriff on *The Andy Griffith Show*. Yatsie used his own car, which was decked out with a red light and a siren bolted to the fenders. He always parked his car in front of the Solano Theatre on Texas Street, and everyone called him Howard.

In 1943, Rex Clift became the sole officer (and chief) when Fairfield had 1,600 residents. While public drunkenness and other minor offenses were the norm, Clift's department did solve several bank robberies. When the police dispatcher wanted to get ahold of beat cops downtown, they would

Fairfield police cruisers on Texas Street in Fairfield. *Fairfield Police Department Facebook page.*

turn on the red light above the downtown Fairfield sign like the Bat Signal. Clift died at the age of forty-two of a sudden heart attack in 1958 and was such a beloved member of the community that five years later there was an effort to have the second high school (Fairfield High) named Rex Clift High School. Eventually, Rex Clift Lane, where the Art Koch Training facility is located, was named in his honor.

From very humble beginnings, the Fairfield Police Department has grown into a modern entity serving the needs of over 120,000 residents.

Q&A WITH RETIRED FAIRFIELD POLICE SERGEANT CHUCK TIMM

According to Wikipedia, The Six Degrees of Kevin Bacon is a parlor game where players challenge each other to arbitrarily choose an actor and then connect them to another actor via a film that both actors have appeared in together, repeating this process to find the shortest path that ultimately leads to prolific American actor Kevin Bacon. It rests on the assumption that anyone involved in the Hollywood film industry can be linked through their film roles to Bacon within six steps. The game's name is a reference to "six degrees of separation," a concept that posits that any two people on earth are six or fewer acquaintance links apart.

Well, retired Fairfield Police Sergeant Chuck Timm is the Kevin Bacon of local true crime stories. Of course, part of the reason for that is that he held positions as both the press information officer and the supervisor of investigations.

Timm was an Air Force brat who often moved growing up, and his father ended up at Travis Air Force Base in 1971. Timm wanted to be an Air Force fighter pilot but was betrayed by his less than 20-20 eyesight. He was hired as a police cadet and later became an officer.

He met his future wife, Pat, when they were both attending Vanden High School, and their English teacher was Harry Price, later longtime Fairfield mayor and eventually Timm's city council colleague. When Price asked him to be in a production of the play *You Can't Take It with You*, Timm balked, as he was a sports star not a thespian. But when Price showed him one of the leading ladies, Timm said, "Whoa. Soon it was enter stage right." They wed in 1975.

Q You started out on patrol back in the day, correct?

A Yes, I was a patrol officer and had a beat. Back then we had a boss that wanted guys prowling the back alleys looking for burglars. He wanted us to not just drive up and down the main drag but to get into our beats and know it. Back then, we thought it sucked, and we felt like we were security guards, but that was actually pretty progressive back then. He was ahead of his time because bad guys don't just go up and down North Texas Street. The job was 95 percent boring with 5 percent sheer terror because you didn't know what the next call was going to be.

Q You are in the HBO Max *Betrayal* episode about the Priscilla Strole murder. What can you tell me about that case?

A I'll never forget that call. That was the most brutal homicide I ever went to. Before that, I had been to a few shootings and afterward maybe fifty or sixty murder scenes, but never one that brutal. The call came out as a woman not breathing. I had a rookie officer, and I told him as we rode there that if

Fairfield Police Sergeant Jim Furco (*left*) and Sergeant Chuck Timm at the Priscilla Strole murder scene. *Public domain.*

she wasn't breathing, he had to do the mouth and I would do the chest. We got there, and Strole's teenage son was out front yelling she couldn't breathe. We went in, and she was on the floor between a coffee table and a couch.

I went down to one knee, and it was kind of dark in there. There may have been a lamp on, but I turned on my flashlight and saw that she…didn't have a face. So, instantly I knew it was a violent act, not just a lady not breathing, and she hadn't been dead long. In that situation, the hairs on your neck go up and you think, "Who did this and where are they?" So now you have to search the house. Think of every scary movie where the person jumps out and makes you shriek. Now imagine you're the guy going down the hall looking for the person who is going to make you shriek.

Q How do they train you for that? Seeing someone without a face?

A You don't get used to it: you get immune. You shut off your emotions because you have a job to do. It takes its toll. You do what you have to do then later you shed a tear and then you're "10-8 and rolling." That means you're ready for another call.

Q When did you meet your partner, Officer Art Koch?

A We were hired around the same time. We had worked together since 1981, when they put us in the Crime Reduction Unit that dealt with gang suppression activity. The day he was killed, I wasn't there. That was his last night on the street before he was being promoted. I had taken off a few days before because it was going to be my last night on the street also, as I was going into detectives. I was in the mountains of New Mexico helping my dad build his retirement house.

His death was a tough pill to swallow for a long time.

We knew Verketis, as we had arrested him half a dozen times. We got along with him fine. I remember one night we put him on the hood of the car so we could talk to him eye to eye. I don't know what set him off that day.

Q Another well-known Fairfield true crime story you were involved in was the Amanda Nikki Campbell case. What do you recall about the night she disappeared?

A That's still an open case, so I have to be kind of careful about what I say. I was the investigation sergeant. It was the twenty-seventh of December 1991, and it was raining. It was my wedding anniversary, so I was getting ready to go home and take my wife out to dinner. An officer pops his head into my office and says we have a missing girl from Salisbury. I figured she was with her grandmother or friends or something, but then time went on and it was 9:00 p.m. and I knew that something was up. We organized searches, and I got home like a day later.

Q What can you tell me about the suspect Timothy Bindner?

A I always said that in a crime investigation, it's like poker and you are given five cards and have to make the best hand. Bindner's name came up because he had a prior contact with a young girl from Fairfield who he was writing letters to who it turned out lived near Amanda Campbell. He was also a suspect in several other cases in the Bay Area.

He would initiate contact with us and taunt us. He kept poking the bear. He's still alive. I think he lives in the Bay Area. In the book *Stalemate*, he told the author, John Philpin, that the reason he flunked a polygraph test was that he was drunk, scared and guilty. The DA said they needed more evidence and so we are still trying to make our best hand. It's frustrating and perplexing. Cops don't forget. If someone kills a police officer, we never forget. If someone kidnaps and kills a little girl, do you think we're going to fold our tent and go away? Hell no.

Q When and how did you become aware of Matt Garcia?

A In 2007, I had been retired two years, and there were a ton of us running for city council. I didn't give Matty a second thought. Then one day my daughter came home, and she

Chuck Timm and Matt Garcia in the council chambers. *The Matt Garcia Foundation.*

said she saw this kid out in front of Starbucks and his name was Matt Garcia and he's running for city council. Then my wife comes home and says something about him. But I knew that this kid had something going for him when one of my best friends, a neighbor who used to work the Iron Triangle in Richmond for the Contra Costa County Sheriff's Department who was an old, grizzled patrol sergeant said "Chuck, I met this kid…"

So I called up Matt and said let's go get some coffee and talk. I said, "You teach me about young Hispanics and I'll teach you about old white guys." We just clicked. We both got elected.

He was just so charismatic. I remember once we went to Grange Middle School to shoot some hoops. I was wearing shorts and sneaks but Matty, like always, was dressed to the nines and he was running circles around the kids, and they loved him. He spoke their language and didn't talk at them, but to them.

Q I realize that you have a lot of rough memories from your time on the police force, but do you have any that were positive, even poignant?

A Yes. During the downtown cruise we received a call of a baby not breathing at the roller rink, and I was like a block away, and even with red lights and sirens there was nowhere to go because of the bumper-to-bumper traffic. So, I remember driving the last one hundred yards or so down the sidewalk. I went running in, and it turned out it wasn't a baby; it was a sixteen-year-old girl. She was on the floor dead, and we started CPR and brought her back. They didn't know what had happened to her.

About six months later, she was walking through the quad at Fairfield High and she just keeled over. The school resource officer was right there and did CPR and brought her back. They found out she had a congenital heart defect where it would kind of like just turn the ignition switch off. They gave her something like a fancy pacemaker that could tell when that was going to happen and would shock her heart. Long story short, I was in her wedding and I'm the godfather to her first daughter.

Chuck Timm in the Fairfield City Council Chamber. *Public domain.*

8
THE LIGHTER SIDE OF LOCAL LAWBREAKING

Researching and writing my first four books for The History Press was a fun, if sometimes tedious process. It was always great to learn something new and I relished the idea of people enjoying them later. To be sure, I write for me, as I have to be satisfied first, but if others enjoy them all the better.

The common thread of those first four books was the intoxicating aroma of nostalgia that often had readers meeting me halfway with their own memories. At a book signing, a guy walked up, opened a copy of *Growing Up in Vacaville* and proceeded to flip through pages with a wonderful smile and an occasional chuckle or deep musical sigh that expressed affection for a long past restaurant, business or event. The guy didn't even buy a copy of the book, yet he still made my day with his reactions.

Doing the research for this book was markedly different from my previous experiences.

For example, I knew Matt Garcia and was going to call him on September 2, 2008, the day I learned he had been shot. It was emotionally difficult to revisit that very dark time.

In the cases where I didn't know the victim, it was still hard. There were many times after reading the details about a murder that I just needed to decompress by watching internet cat videos or an episode or two of *Seinfeld*.

In the event many of y'all share that experience after reading this book, I decided to add this chapter. It still focuses on true crimes but ones pulled from past newspapers that were a little (or a lot) less awful than those highlighted in the previous chapters. As with all cases in this book, they do have a connection to Fairfield, even if it is time spent in the county jail downtown.

BUMBLING BURGLARY: FEBRUARY 5, 1953

Karl's Drive In, not Carl's Jr., was located on Highway 40 near where Texas Roadhouse now sits. According to then Sheriff Tommy Joyce, burglars broke in and stole cigarettes and cash from a vending machine and attempted to force open a safe. They also stole three boxes of cigars and a portable typewriter (?).

Officers saw evidence that the thieves parked in a car two hundred yards away and evidently had to push-start their getaway car.

PANTIE RAID: NOVEMBER 9, 1953

At Waterman Park, a pantie raid "similar to those on Southern California colleges" took place in Waterman Park, the federal military housing complex that was later razed to make way for the Fairfield community center complex.

A resident there reported the theft of four nylon slips, twelve pairs of nylon panties and other unmentionables. The complainant said her

Unmentionables on a clothesline. *Pixabay.*

husband's clothing had been hanging right next to hers, but they had not been disturbed.

Yeah, that's because boxer or tightie-whitie raiding wasn't a thing in 1953—and it ain't a thing now either.

Driver Arrested After Wild Chase: March 19, 1959

Suisun City police saw a 1947 car making a speedy exit from the city onto the highway at about 3:00 a.m. and gave chase. At the Grizzly Island cutoff, the driver turned off his lights, but the police car's spotlight kept the car in sight as they chased him, reaching speeds of up to ninety miles per hour.

The chase ended in the driveway of the John Lawler property. The driver bailed and took off on foot in the open fields. An officer called for the man to halt and then, as was the dubious practice back then, fired a warning shot over his head. Police found the man, a twenty-three-year-old airman from Travis Air Force base, in the field.

The kicker was after all that—car chase, foot pursuit and warning shot—he was still holding a glass with whiskey in it.

A perp gets chased, shot at and still manages to hold onto his glass of whiskey. *Pixabay.*

Cookie Theft Charged to Eleven-Year-Old Boy: March 22, 1959

Fairfield police were dispatched to the downtown Food Fair market where an eleven-year-old boy was nabbed trying to take a package of cookies without paying for them. When the police arrived, they found the boy crying in the market because the cookies had been taken from him.

An illustration of the downtown Fairfield Food Fair. *Fairfield Civic Center Library microfilm.*

He was released to the custody of his mother but not easily. The Baked Goods Bandit had to be restrained by an officer en route to the police department as he tried to jump from the squad car.

Now his compulsion to pilfer the cookies might be somewhat understandable if they had been irresistible Double Stuf Oreos, but those weren't introduced until 1974, so his behavior was completely inexplicable.

HOME HAIRCUT STARTS SPREE AT GUN CLUB: MARCH 26, 1959

Now, where do you even start with a headline like that? How are those things even remotely related?

Here's how: A twelve-year-old Cordelia boy decided to cut his own hair for some reason, and the results were, predictably, less than stellar. He figured he should make himself scarce before his dad got home so he took his six-year-old stepbrother with him and kicked the door open to the Pierce Gun Club near Nelson's Quarry.

They cooked something to eat and then looked around for something to amuse themselves.

They found some shotgun ammunition and decided to bake it in the stove. Although it exploded, the boys miraculously escaped injury.

When discovered, they were burning matches for lack of anything better to do.

Their kid logic of trying to avoid a punishment for an offense by doing something much worse seems ridiculous on the surface but is actually quite ingenious. It's a tried-and-true method of diversion. It's similar to, say, a twenty-two-year-old who sits his parents down and tells them he has terminal cancer. Once they are sufficiently saddened, shocked and worried, he says, "I don't actually have cancer. I'm just gay."

THE GREAT CHICKEN FAT THEFT: JANUARY 26, 1968

It's always refreshing to come across articles in microfilm where it's obvious the reporters had fun writing. Take for instance, this story that was on the front page of the *Daily Republic*:

> *Fairfield police may have solved the local crime of the century—The Great Chicken Fat Robbery.*
>
> *The mystery has reportedly left some frying pans greaseless for the past two years.*
>
> *Nicholas G. Stavros, 21 from Manteca, was booked in Solano County Jail for theft. He admitted planning to take a 50 gallon drum of chicken fat from behind Foster's Old-Fashion Freeze* [where Yo Sushi is now located].
>
> *The Peterson Tallow Company of Emeryville owned the drums, not the fat and company officials were summoned to identify barrels found in Stavros' truck. Over 200 of the company's large metal drums have been taken in Fairfield and other Bay Area cities.*
>
> *Police were staked out close to Foster's Freeze at 3:30 a.m. when Stavros reportedly drove into the lot, cut his lights and removed a grease barrel from a fenced-in area behind the drive-in restaurant. Collared by officers, he said he planned to take the barrel but "changed his mind."*
>
> *Today with Stavros behind bars, chicken fat users are breathing a little easier.*

BEAUTY SCHOOL BREAK-INS: JULY 5, 1968

A string of burglaries occurred in Fairfield at the Fairfield Beauty Academy, where fifty dollars was taken, and Pagoda Hair Fashions, where no losses were reported. A similar break-in happened at the Vallejo Beauty Academy.

If ever there was a time when I wanted to reach back through time and slap someone for trying to be too clever, it would be the *Daily Republic* editor who branded the article about the break-ins "Police Search for 'Jack the Clipper.'"

DRUNKENNESS CHARGED TO TWO MEN IN ALLEY: AUGUST 3, 1968

Now the particulars of this incident are not really that compelling; two Travis Air Force Base airmen were arrested for public drunkenness, disturbing the peace and resisting arrest. The interesting fact is that one of them was also charged with "using profanity in front of a woman."

I have some questions.

What constitutes profanity? I mean, is there a list of words similar to George Carlin's "7 Words You Can Never Say on Television?" Is it like that Supreme Court justice who said something similar about pornography—that he knows it when he sees it? Could a woman be charged with detonating F-bombs in front of another woman? I need to know.

BURGLAR TAKES TIME TO COOK BREAKFAST: DECEMBER 20, 1968

This one is damn peculiar.

John Hollingsworth of Rio Vista reported to the sheriff's office that while he was visiting Lodi, someone broke into his house and stole a tin can that had $110 (close to $1,000 in 2025) in it.

Peculiar thing 1: Hollingsworth came home and went to bed and in the morning went to the kitchen to prepare breakfast. When he got there, he found that the table was already set and had been used. Someone had used the frying pan to cook an omelet, set the table and eaten the meal.

Peculiar thing 2: Hollingsworth understandably got nervous and started checking to see if anything was missing. That's when he discovered his money can was gone. He called the sheriff and reported the theft.

Peculiar thing 3: Later in the day, when Hollingsworth was about to use his washing machine, he found his tin can in it. He called the police back because the thief, for some reason, had hidden it there after taking only $30.

A nice touch was that the writer of the newspaper article noted that even though the thief set the table, cooked an omelet and ate it, that "the inconsiderate person left without washing the dishes."

Boy Robbed by Girls: August 3, 1974

In Suisun City, three girls, ages ten to eleven, held up an eight-year-old boy as he was returning home from the market.

The victim was returning from the Short Stop after having been given $5 to purchase two large bottles of soda. That set him back $1.48, so as he was walking home with the change (which would be over $22 in 2025) he was approached by the Y-chromosome-less trio. "Give me that money" was the only comment before the change was snatched from the boy's hand and he was pushed to the ground.

The police were able to apprehend the three girls based on a description.

Now, this was in 1974, and gender roles being what they were back then, this is the kind of crime where, as the young boy, you would be very grateful that the names of minors, both miscreants and victims, were not published in the newspaper.

AFTERWORD

There is no society known where a more or less developed criminality is not found under different forms. No people exist whose morality is not daily infringed upon. We must therefore call crime necessary and declare that it cannot be non-existent, that the fundamental conditions of social organization, as they are understood, logically imply it.
—Émile Durkheim

I have mined the luscious gold of nostalgia since 2011 in my Back in the Day columns and then in local history books. As a co-admin of the I Grew Up in Fairfield Too Facebook group, I have helped create a space on the social media site that is a controversy-free zone.

We intentionally carved out a spot where arguments about politics, religion and the name-calling and negativity that are the calling cards of cowardly keyboard warriors are strictly verboten. The most controversial things allowed in that Fairfield group is good-natured crosstown rivalry smack talk between Armijo High and Fairfield High alumni and which burger place in Fairfield is the best (the correct answer is Dave's Giant Hamburgers).

Because of the no-controversy rule, some have accused the admins of living with rose-colored goggles permanently affixed to our heads. Nothing could be further from the truth. In fact, many years ago (before we enacted the rule), I challenged several longtimers who attempted to paint a Mayberry-esque picture of past Fairfield. To let them tell it, the worst thing that ever happened was someone got a ticket for letting their downtown parking meter expire.

But for years I have been accumulating digital files of past local newspaper articles from microfilm (I have well over ten thousand now) and have routinely come across true crime stories. There were burglaries, robberies, domestic squabbles and, yes, murders.

Cities are always going to have crime. That's the reason one of the first things local authorities do when any municipality first becomes incorporated as a city is appoint or elect law enforcement officers. Wherever there are people, there are going to be conflicts and crime.

When writing this book, I had to make choices about what to include and what to leave out. It's similar to what newspaper editors and other media sources do all the time. And just like them, I have mixed motivations.

On one level I believe there are stories in this book that simply needed to be told and presented in this manner. However, I also knew that I was not writing a free blog; I was writing a book that I, and The History Press, hope people will buy. So I went through countless stories of Fairfield crimes and gave the greenlight to some and rejected others. My criteria were not as crass as "if it bleeds, it leads" like many TV news stations, but the chosen entries

Downtown Fairfield. *Antoine Dello.*

had to stand out and at the very least be interesting like the proverbial "man bites dog" story.

I think an important point to raise is that our perceptions of how we view a city can be skewed by accounts of the crime there presented in newspapers, on TV or the internet and, yes, in books. I have sometimes been flabbergasted by the reaction of people who moved away from Fairfield years ago and hear about some local crime. They assume that people still residing in Fairfield are all issued mandatory flak jackets and are dodging bullets 24/7. That ain't happenin'.

It reminds me of when I helped with a Matt Garcia Foundation spring cleanup at Allan Witt Park in 2021. When I drove into the park, there were a few homeless people who had tents near the picnic area. I don't recall ever seeing homeless people in the park or anywhere else while growing up in Fairfield. (Well, we used to wave to "hobos" on the trains that ran behind our house, but that's the exception that proves the rule.)

But you know what else I saw at the park that day? Kids playing basketball in the gym and on the outside courts. Almost every single softball diamond being used. Skateboarding in the skate park. Families with dogs playing Frisbee. In short, the everyday life of members of a community enjoying a municipal asset. Sure, Fairfield has problems, every city does, but it also has a collective beating heart of fundamental goodness.

It's all about what I choose to focus on. I love seeing the spectrum of Fairfield folks lining downtown streets during the annual Fourth of July and Veterans Day parades. There are people of different races, ages, socioeconomic statuses, genders, sexual orientations and faiths (or no faith)—it's a beautiful thing to behold.

Thanks for taking a journey with me in this book, which is about not particularly pleasant events, but please don't get it twisted. I would hate for anyone to miss the beauty of Fairfield just because of the ugliness of some of its trees.

ACKNOWLEDGEMENTS

First I want to thank my in-house editor of five years and wife of thirty years, Beth. I also want to give special thanks to Chuck Timm, Barbara Koch and Elsa Cisneros for sharing remembrances with me. Fist bumps to everyone at The History Press for all their help. Virtual hugs to my Bright Line Eating community that supports me and especially founder Susan Pierce Thompson, PhD, for not only saving my life, but helping me discover the confidence and courage to "pursue the most cherished and long-ago abandoned longings of my heart."

BIBLIOGRAPHY

Books

La Mezcla Yearbooks. Armijo High School, various years.
Munro-Fraser, J.P. *The History of Solano County 1879*. Wood, Alley & Co, 1879.
Philpin, John. *Stalemate: A Shocking True Story of Child Abduction and Murder*. Random House, 1997.
Weir, David. *That Fabulous Captain Waterman*. Comet Press Books, 1957.
Wilson, Colin. *A Criminal History of Mankind*. Granada Publishing Limited, 1984.

Websites

Ancestry.com | https://www.ancestry.com
Historical Articles of Solano County Online Database | http://www.solanoarticles.com
"I Grew Up in Fairfield, Too," Facebook group | https://www.facebook.com/groups/fairfieldyears
Newspapers.com | https://www.newspapers.com
Solano County History Facebook group | https://www.facebook.com/groups/1555977548059196
Solano County Sheriff's Office History Facebook page | https://www.facebook.com/SCSOHistory
Vacaville Heritage Council | www.https://www.vacavilleheritagecouncil.org/.

Other

Solano Republican/Daily Republic microfilm, Fairfield Civic Center Library
Vacaville Reporter microfilm, Vacaville Cultural Center Library

ABOUT THE AUTHOR

Tony Wade came to Fairfield in 1976, when he was twelve years old, and never left. In 2006, Wade began writing columns for the local newspaper, *The Daily Republic*, as a freelance writer.

In 2011, Wade became an accidental historian when he began writing his Back in the Day columns, which he describes as "kinda, sorta about local history." He has now written over seven hundred of them.

Wade has authored four previous books for The History Press: *Growing Up in Fairfield, California* (2021), *Lost Restaurants of Fairfield, California* (2022), *Armijo High School: Fairfield, California* (2023) and *Growing Up in Vacaville* (2024).

In 2024, California State Senator Bill Dodd presented Wade with a resolution commending him for his community service and his humorous and historical writings. He was honored but a little disappointed they didn't include his dozen years volunteering for the Fairfield Fourth of July and Veterans Day parades—he wanted to have the first resolution with the words "pooper scooper" on it.

He lives in Fairfield with his wife and in-house editor, Beth, and their Chiweenie, Chunky Tiberius Wade.

Visit Tony Wade's website www.tonywadeaccidentalhistorian.com and shoot him an email at toekneeweighed@gmail.com.